MW00638790

MONT*ANA*

*Growing-up the youngest of 16 children
in a wild, rambunctious and poor
family, Margie creatively entertains
and educates us with unforgettable
heartwarming and healing stories.*

WIFE

Painted by 8 year old son, Kevin Johnson

MARGIE JOHNSON

Printed and bound in the United States of America
First printing • ISBN # 978-1-7345637-9-5
Copyright © 2020

MARGIE JOHNSON

FOR ORDER INFORMATION VISIT
www.scottcompanypublishing.com/store

SCOTT PUBLISHING COMPANY
www.scottpublishingcompany.com
P.O. Box 9707 • Kalispell, MT 59904
Toll Free: 1-800-628-0212
Fax: 1-406-756-0098

TABLE OF CONTENTS

DEDICATION

This book is dedicated to our two grandsons, Conner and Cody. (Of course we call you Major and Colonel because you rank so high in our lives!)

This is our legacy to you.

Love Grandma J and Papa J

WHY I WROTE THIS BOOK

From the depths of a disadvantaged childhood, to the heights of extraordinary wealth, Margie Johnson is blessed. And she knows it.

The last of sixteen children, Margie grew up with very little. Taking her many, many childhood disadvantages, she made them her adult opportunities! She claims a person's character is built out of her crisis and that's how she becomes inwardly rich.

Her family roots cleanly trace to Montana pioneers. Margie's grandfather, Charles Wesley Hutton, moved to Libby in 1894 and became Libby's first school principal in 1899. Margie married, had two sons, lost one when he was 9, later gained a daughter-in-law and two grandsons, started a business and lives today in Libby, Montana with her spouse of 51 years, Junior, on 10 wooded acres of her family's original 160-acre homestead.

That's the big picture. Here's the rest of the story:

Sadly, Margie's parents separated when she was 6 years old. For 7 years, until she was 13 (what should have been formative years) and her parents reunited, Margie and her older 8-year-old and 11-year-old siblings lived completely alone because her mother worked out of town. During this difficult time, Margie learned valuable lessons in self-reliance and expresses gratitude for the ultimate positive effects these troubled years had on her life.

Through the fog of daily survival, Margie also understood the value of education. She doggedly attended school and was one of just three in her family to finish high school. Contrite, Margie conceded her degree as partly gratis given her poor marks. Such tenacity, however, best characterizes her endurance through those early years as well as in all future endeavors.

Successful people often make more good choices than bad. Margie's mate is arguably her best. Junior is an honorable man from humble roots. Together, they grew through the early married years establishing the prosperity that defines them today.

Margie's wealth is based on faith in God, not money. At 22, she began formal Bible study and was glad the initial education was private. Amusedly, she says her first question after hearing the Adam and Eve story was, "What was their last name?" Today, Margie is a speaker for women's conferences and retreats.

The sudden, unexpected loss of their younger son Kevin 9 years later tested them severely. The autopsy proved cancer - lymphoma of the small intestine - not an appendectomy gone wrong. Until two weeks before his death there were no illness indications. Several doctor visits failed to reveal any issue. Alas, doctor's eventually opined the fast-growing tumor would allow only 3-5 months more life.

In retrospect, Margie believes they were not given more than they could endure.

Over the ten years following the death of their son Margie wrote "Death is a Promise; Not a Problem." Published in 1999, this book discusses their loss, chronicles Kevin's death, and describes their strengthened joy and peace. No reader can fail to feel the depth of Margie's convictions and the breadth of her spiritual wealth.

Initially, Margie wrote as a cathartic response to a painful life event. She found it therapeutic to put her pain in print. People responded to her story, writing, and pain. Dr. Neil Gallagher, Ph.D. and author, hailed Death is a Promise; Not a Problem as a "...gentle, dramatic, inspirational, well-written book."

An obviously talented writer, Margie next wrote "Teaching Spiritual Values from Tots to Teens," also published in 1999. Her creative approach to making magical moments with children further define Margie's crystal clear appreciation of life's truest treasures.

Margie is expressive, creative, and inventive in s-o-o-o many directions! She gives herself away in numerous articles written over years to national publication Christian Woman Magazine. Many of these articles address decorating on a dime.

Margie relates all her passions or "sweet spots" to helping others... even decorating! She believes everyone appreciates and is proud of a well decorated home that is organized and always welcoming. Because of her poor living conditions growing up, she especially believes a child's self-image is affected. And for that reason, she created a business affordable to most who want their home decorated at very little cost. Her business has also taken her to homes where money is no problem.

Since starting her business, Decorating on a Dime, she has successfully garnered the attention of clients in and out of Montana. She decorated homes in Texas, California, Idaho and Washington. Her own home was decorated on a dime.

She has even reached out and decorated restaurants, a spa and a financial business. But whether decorating for business owners or homeowners, whether they have modest means or are millionaires, Margie approaches all with equal excitement and enthusiasm. She offers an impressive array of style options and is sensitive to client needs, wants and desires.

In addition to teaching others how to decorate on a dime, Margie is equally adept at dining and dressing on a dime, and loves sharing this expertise with others. One of the traveling workshops she presents, "Holiday Hospitality," teaches participants how to, "be the hostess with the mostest for the leastest."

Coming from such a huge family, with well over a hundred nieces and nephews, Margie extends her hospitality by bringing the girl cousins back to their Montana roots every five years to help keep them all connected. She hosts a Montana Cousin Chick Party, right after Easter. The gals all pack their suitcase, fluff their feathers, fly in from all over United States and roost at local hotels.... just to keep connected and keep the little girl in them.

Margie is one of the wealthiest Montana women one could meet, and equally unassuming. She readily accepts the fact that she is a work in progress and relishes every opportunity for self-growth. A philanthropist at heart, she shares her wealth on a daily basis through personal interface, her written words and the many hearts she's touched along her path. Margie encourages us all to live every day with those we love, like it's our last, and make as few regrets as possible.

(This was taken from Montana Woman Magazine, Susan Rhein interviewed me.)

My Beginnings

Wild Child

MY VIEW FROM THE FRONT PORCH

My Montana mother had nine boys and seven girls. I am the youngest of 16 children. I was always glad she never stopped with 15. But notice our two family photos. One was when we were younger and the other when we were older. Unfortunately, neither photo has us all together at the same time. So, there's no need to count!

I want to share some of my immediate siblings' stories. First, understand this about big families: the story version changes, depending on who is talking and seeing it from their own perspective. So, by my being the youngest and seeing it from the bottom of the nest, my version becomes just as valid as from the top.

But speaking of my being the last, I remember my last laughs with my 80-year-old mother. The year before she died, she was at my home for supper. Watching me stir gravy, she commented, "You stir gravy just like I did. Your Dad always teased that I wiggled while I stirred." Triggering my humor, I turned around, pumping my eyebrows and asked, "So was I your sixteenth pan of gravy?"

That true story is just to warn you that from here on, everything I share is either from my own memory or family hearsay or just a whole lot of fun, meaning some is true and some is exaggerated, but it's all meant to be enjoyed.

I remember we lived so far out in the woods that we had to go towards town to go hunting.

Our two-story ranch home had a front porch. I've decided parents of big families built those porches for sanity reasons. In the good old days, when parents had 8, 10, 12, or 16 little curtain climbers to deal with indoors on rainy days, they couldn't scream, "Get outside and play!" So, some smart mom and dad at wit's end started lifting lumber and pounding nails and setting roofing on the front-end of their homes and making it possible to herd kids outdoors to play in all weather elements. I am sure that is why front porches were invented.

Instead of a WELCOME sign, my parents posted a sign warning, BEWARE OF KIDS. I think they got the idea from that old movie, Ma and Pa Kettle. I always liked that movie. I could relate! Actually, I thought they were some long lost relatives that made it big in Hollywood. Besides, when you come from our big family, you think you are related to the whole world. The first time I heard the Bible story about Adam and Eve, I wanted to know their last name… seriously.

Speaking of the Bible, my parents raised us with no religion. I had absolutely no Bible knowledge until I was older. One day I remember trying to retell the story of Sodom and Gonorrhea! I got my high school health class mixed up with my adult Bible study.

At Ranch on River on front porch
brother Cleve in back, sister Shirley, sister Marcia holding niece Cathy,
nephew Steve, sister Audith, Margie

But back to our front porch: There was actually a doghouse dug out underneath. I figured even dogs get overwhelmed and start digging a grave when there are that many rambunctious kids. I remember the doghouse read, KEEP OUT! But we kids liked being in the doghouse. He had more room than we did.

Eventually our crowded front porch became roomier because six of my nine brothers joined the military. They wanted to get away from the fighting.

Our kitchen was the first room you entered in our home. The aroma of homemade bread filled the air as my mother mixed up a batch of bread dough for 27 loaves each week. The breadbox was a family heirloom passed down to me. To this day, I still lift the lid and can smell my mom's homemade bread, buns and cinnamon rolls. This family breadbox was a 30-gallon galvanized garbage can. My mom had no need for a garbage can. With that many kids there is never garbage.

The Waltons on TV were a more fortunate family than we. They all got a place at the dinner table. Our dinnertime was like musical chairs. I remember if you missed getting a chair, then you had to sit on the adjoining staircase. Your dinner plate on your knees became your TV tray. Oh, and we had no television. Just watching each other was entertaining enough. Besides, we had no electricity.

But I never understood my friends' parents. They said they grew up with their folks harping at the dinner table, "If you take it, you eat it." At our house we were applauded, "If you got it, you get it!" My fattest brother always got a standing ovation.

We kids did have some manners. Not having indoor plumbing, we were always taught to be polite and save the Sears catalog's soft, yellow pages for company.

Speaking of politeness, when my oldest brother went to school, he wasn't trying to be a smart mouth, but when the teacher had him use the word, "depot" in a sentence, he wrote, "We put depot under de' bed at night."

Thank goodness we had indoor bathing. Our big round galvanized steel bathtub sat in the middle of our kitchen floor next to the wood cook stove. Being the youngest, they started bathing me first, and the oldest was last. And we only got our turn once a week. I am making us sound like a bunch of rednecks. But we weren't. We never scrubbed that hard.

Beds were sparse. So sparse if we had company, they pulled out a bottom dresser drawer for me to sleep in. But normally Mom packed six of us smaller ones crosswise like sardines. I remember, four were "bed wetters" and two of us were swimmers. But as we got older, she put four sisters to a bed--two at the top and two at the bottom. I remember waking up to twenty toes in my face. I never got to sleep alone until after I got married.

There were more kids than animals on the farm, so we included them in the family. In fact, for fun, my older siblings dressed the cows in hats, and sneaking my mom's ruby-red lipstick, smeared the entire tube on their full lips. Actually, I think we were a family ahead of our times. I know for a fact we were great inventors. As I see it, all this desire for injecting Botox for beautiful plump lips today actually started on our family farm.

In the good old days, farm kids had clever ways to invent fun. And I remember how the cows in the pasture made a great audience. They stood and chewed their cud endlessly as I twirled my baton or jumped rope. And all the cackling chickens perched in the chicken coop made up the first orchestra I conducted.

And what a treat it was to go to school. You didn't have to deal with so many kids.

That reminds me. It was in school when I heard for the first time the nursery rhyme about an "old lady who lived in a shoe ... she had so many children she didn't know what to do." Seriously, I thought it was a cartoon about our family! And as a first grader, I thought I was one smart little girl and was about to pass her first test. I could see the flaw ... the illustrator made a mistake ... the shoe had no front porch!

NONE OF US ARE SO POOR
WE CAN'T AFFORD TO LAUGH

Do you ever wake-up in the middle of the night thinking about your parents? Mine passed away many years ago, but I still think of them often. In fact, my funniest memory of them entertained me just the other night at 3:42 AM, to be exact.

I was the youngest of 16 children. My parents Evelyn and Harold Hutton, (also known as Happy Hutton - hmm, I wonder why?) were old-timers in Libby, Montana. My mother, having had sixteen children in twenty-three years, prided herself in never owning a maternity dress or baby bottle. Along with my dad if he was home to help, she delivered fourteen of us sixteen babies. Being a staunch German, she was actually arrogant about the fact that her double-knotted belly buttons from using sterilized string were, as she loudly put it, "better than today's new fangled clamps!" Seriously, those were her reprimanding words

Evelyn and Harold Hutton - 1967

with her pointed finger under my doctor's nose after our first son was born in 1969.

All that is said to lead up to my Dad's distinctive personality. Quite the opposite! He was quiet. Not a noisy man at all. In fact, for my mother, he was painfully quiet because he could go days without saying a word. However, listening closely, one could hear his dry sense of humor.

So, with it being 3:42 A.M. and wide-awake, I remembered my mother telling one of the times he made her laugh. She went to work on a graveyard shift when I was very young. However, one particular work-night she didn't like having to leave the farm because one of her piglets was ill. (Baby chicks and piglets were her very favorite). But having to go regardless, she said, "Early the very next morning when I got home, and even though I was dog-tired, I ran down the hill to the pigpen to see if my piglet was still alive. I was surprised he was. I took him up to the house and, taking water from the reservoir on the wood cook-stove, I filled my old white enamel bowl and scrubbed him down good. Then I pinned your cloth diaper on him and snuggled him in bed with me and went to sleep. Later your Dad walked in and saw us in bed and asked, 'Are we having pigs now?'"

That story embarrassed me as a teenager. Because of peer pressure and thinking totally of myself, I thought it made us seem so hillbilly or redneck as a family. But now that I am older and more appreciative, I am proud of my family heritage. Maybe my Montana parents weren't important in the community and we weren't anything like that model TV family, The Waltons. But both of my parents astound me with the sacrificial love they showed for sixteen of us little newborns, making sure we took our first breath and then feeding, sheltering and clothing us all. Obviously, they would have done it even for a baby pig.

"Lord, for that reason bless my mother and bless my dad. They were hard working Montana folks. I should have been saying these prayers for them many years before, and I wasn't. But thanks for helping me realize it now. And also, thanks for waking me up at this hour to understand how refreshing that humor must have been for my mother and that she could set aside for a moment the worry of so many little mouths to feed. And forgive me for my selfish embarrassment, for I now truly understand the old saying, 'Laughter is good medicine.' Amen."

My mother's shopping trip to town with 11 children - 1950

14 siblings with 2 missing - 1991

MONTANA DREAMS DIDN'T ALWAYS COME EASY

Sitting on my front porch, this sad story won't leave me alone. It's about my neighbors. Well actually they were my grandparents' and parents' neighbors starting in the early 1900s. They homesteaded next door, and I now live on 10 acres of our family's original homestead. Between my mother telling me about this Montana woman she knew and my reading about her, you too will feel a sense of sadness, because not all Montana women's dreams come easy. For the sake of the family, the homesteaders' names are not mentioned.

Back on a small plot of timbered land is a fenced family cemetery. Carved out of the original family homestead, it only holds three souls, a mother and her two daughters. Just yesterday I stood before this family burial plot with the forest's fallen debris at my feet. Leaning over, I wiped off the headstones like any loving mother would wipe the tears from her child's face. Having lost a child myself, I had the feeling this is what their mother would have wanted me to do.

The mother, whom I'll call Mary, had a dream along with her husband to file for a homestead 8 miles outside of Libby, Montana. Granted the 160 acres, they had to show proof of improving the land. Cutting logs, the family (consisting of Mary, her husband and five children) built a cabin on the creek frontage the first year. The oldest child, a daughter, had left the family home by then. The next year, their dream drove them to build an oversized barn and root cellar. Improvements were being made.

By the end of the second year this Montana woman found herself married to a man whose dream had dissolved. He no longer wanted to keep doing the back-bending work and improving upon the land. Without going into details, it was at that time they received tragic news that their oldest daughter died. Mary had their daughter buried on the homestead. After her husband's change of heart and loss of their daughter, their marriage dissolved. Mary, now with her deceased daughter buried on the land, was more determined than ever to stay with her dream and improve the land.

Now being a single mom with two older sons and three younger daughters, she forged forward to improve her homestead. However shortly the oldest son left home. That left Mary with one son bearing the workload with her. Then one late August, another family tragedy struck. The baby sister died before medical attention could reach her. The only brother at home had to dig a second grave. He then walked the 8 miles to town and carried her small coffin back home on his back.

I can only imagine this younger son by then had done a lot of thinking. Because as it turned out, he too, in his grief and discouragement, wanted no more part of the homestead dream. He moved away next. Again, regardless, Mary stayed.

My grandfather Charles W. Hutton was a teacher (remember my family were neighbors), and taught the oldest daughter in his nearby one-room log school until she was in the eighth and last grade at the rural school. She then moved to town to attend school.

Now Mary was truly alone, with only her one daughter. The work now consisted of milking one cow in an over-sized barn, tending to a small garden, burning brush, taking a hatchet to tree stumps and doing whatever it takes to show improvement to her homestead dream.

Then a promise came into her life. A man hopped off the train and walked into Libby's local saloon. In a short time, engaged in a conversation and looking for work, he was directed to helping homesteaders, which led to Mary. Mary liked his work ethic - plus he was attracted to her! That was flattering, minus the fact he was young enough to be her son. Long story short, she got pregnant. He got a draft call and WWI took him to France. When he came home he married the hardworking homestead woman who was raising their one-year-old child.

After the war, the requirements for "improving your land" were finally completed. Mary's first love, the homestead land, belonged to her. But her second marriage to the younger man no longer did. They ended in divorce. And again, through that, she stayed on her homestead. She lived there until 1942. That was the year she admitted she was unable to live there alone.

Mary passed away in 1947 and was buried by her two daughters in the little homestead graveyard. That was her request. And it was honored.

She had a dream. It didn't come easy. But the bottom line is, because of her tenacity, she actually fulfilled it.

Marriage & Romance

WILD WIFE AND HER WEAPON

Hunting season was coming and Junior did not want to shave, yet he wanted his hugs. I pleaded with him to please shave. I explained how his stubbly face was torment on my soft skin. He just ignored my request. You woman know what I am talking about.

However, being ignored by my husband brings out this wild woman part in me!

So, as usual, climbing into bed, I could see this porcupine drawing near to me. I went into a defense mode. I gingerly slid away and found my footing as I slipped out of bed. With both feet on the ground and not giving any eye contact, I knew I needed a plan. I slowly backed over to the nearby dresser and got my weapon. I held it close to my side. Then to confuse this wild animal…I smiled and slid back in bed. As he once again approached me, I knew I had set a trap. A trap that would stop him.

And sure enough when this beast with quills came in for the kissing and hugging, I quickly withdrew my mammoth, round, prickly hairbrush from my side. I swiped him again and again! It was a clean kill to his emotions. He jumped effortlessly out of bed and yelped, "What was that?"

I proudly held up my beautiful, bristly hairbrush. I even blew off the smoke like you would a hot pistol. Then with my messy hair standing-up like hackles and eyes of fire, he knew, (better said…he felt) don't mess with this wild wife of yours until you shave.

MISTAKEN IDENTITY... REALLY?

Take a close look at that photo.

First, bless you Montana Women who others think your daughter is your sister. But what about us who are mistaken for our husband's mother? Has that ever happened to you? Well, it continually happens to me.

It started back when our son Travis was in high school working at a fast-food place. Standing opposite Travis at the counter, the cook hollered, "Your mom and brother's order is ready!" Well, my husband ate that up! ... enjoying his first happy meal.

The next time it happened Travis was in college. We drove to his campus and his friends were certain that Mom brought big brother to visit younger brother. Again, my husband gloated. I debated whether to leave campus or leave my husband's swollen head attached to his body. Well, because he is my meal ticket, I left him intact.

Speaking of a swollen head, I briefly had one in New York City. Staying in Times Square, we went shopping for the touristy t-shirt reading 'Big Apple'. The shop owner, who appeared to be Greek or Italian and a very intense man, interrupted the t-shirt decision by asking, "Madam, are those your green eyes?"

"Yes," I replied with a smile.

"No, really, really, are those your green eyes?" asking with both his hands making those little come-on circles like some delightfully expressive Italians do.

"Yeah!" I smiled now even bigger.

"Beautiful! Beautiful!!" He emphatically exclaimed now with both

Junior with his Wildflower, July 2006

hands raised high above his head.

"Well, thank you," I humbly responded, adding, "You make me feel very good."

Turning to Junior, my husband, the intense man took his flying arms from above his head and struck my husband in the mid-drift, chastising, "Don't you tell your momma every day she has beautiful eyes?" So from small town Montana to New York City, I am thought to be my husband's mother.

Speaking of big city, recently it happened again at Chicago's O'Hare airport. Talking with a quite elderly gentleman about his interesting career as a boxing referee, I had a ton of questions because my dad had been a boxing fan. Junior, who is normally the noisier mate between the two of us, never spoke. He was never exposed to boxing. The man finally asked, pointing, "Is this your son?"

"No, actually," I calmly replied, "he is my youngest great grandson."

"No-o-o, really?" Like he was complimenting me. That's when I gave him "The Look!" But I could see that wasn't going to be enough. Since I happened to be reading Dr. Michael D. Sedler's book, When to Speak up and When to Shut Up, I waved that in front of him to settle the subject. He got the point. And, of course, I got the pain. And again, Junior got the praise.

Well, enough said. Sometimes a gal needs a friend to laugh with.

Through my many decades of marriage (and I am the younger mate!) I have come to enjoy my husband getting compliments. I guess that's why I had fun with that old fella at O'Hare. Besides, I'm at that "blessed age of confidence" because I find the old adage is true: In our 20's and 30's we worry about what people think of us. In our 40's and 50's we don't worry or care about what people think of us, because in our 60's and 70's we find out they weren't thinking of us at all!

I've decided it's the combination of my husband's fun personality, having a baby-face and having the name Junior that keeps him young. It may be time to call him by his real name, Wilfred Clarence. Nah! Junior Johnson has a nice ring to it. Besides, he's my "happy meal" ticket.

MONTANA COUGAR

I wrote a previous story describing the many times I have been mistaken for my husband's mother. Well, it happened again!

My husband and I had an appointment to have our photo taken for our church directory. And just for the record, this is quite a famous company known for their professionalism.

So, here we are waiting in line and then it's our turn to enter the room for our photo session. At that time, my husband and I were at retiring age. I tell you this right up front because the gal taking our photo was on-the-heels of our age. I mean, we are not talking about excusing a 20 or even 30 year-old gal here.

She directed my husband to sit down in front of that cloudy or faux colored screen they have set up. Then walking over, she removed the chair next to him and signaled me over, instructing, "Mom, come over and stand behind your son."

Gasping, I slapped my hand over my heart and emphatically stated with a frown, "I am not this man's mother! He is not my son!!" And, as you can only imagine, as I was vigorously saying this, my husband was already wearing a mammoth smile that made an ivory keyboard on a baby grand piano look small.

Now, this woman photographer did not apologize like I expected would be in the works. Instead, she raised an eyebrow, and in a mischievously sly and admiring way, stated, "O-oh, you found yourself a boy-toy."

"A what?" I questioned. I was perplexed. I had never heard the term "boy-toy".

But before she could enlighten me on the latest lingo in our culture,

Junior with his tamed Cougar, Kootenai River

my husband interrupted, eagerly inquiring, "Just how old do you think I am?"

Forgetting my astonished reaction, and failing to apologize or answer my question, this gal got all wishy-washy and placed her forehead in her hands and whined to Junior, "Don't do this to me. I don't know? Maybe 35?"

"Thirty-five!!" I again erupted. "Listen, this man and I… I mean the two of us together... between us, made a baby who is now 45 years old, so how could that be?"

Smiling and ignoring my questions and explosive emotions like water off a duck's back, she calmly asked me, "Then would you rather sit in the chair and have him stand behind you?"

Like, where is my apology? I wondered.

I also wanted to wipe off the smile that was still plastered to my husband's young face by suggesting, "How about if boy-toy just sits on my lap, and perhaps I can find a trinket in my purse to entertain him."

Instead, I sat down and clamped my tongue in my teeth. Besides, she and I needed something to agree upon. I would settle with Junior later.

All the way home in the car, Junior kept looking over and pumping his eyebrows, giving me that grin like he was really some young dude.

The next morning while getting ready for church, our son Travis phoned from Arkansas as he usually does on his way to church. From the bathroom I heard my husband say first thing, "Hey, Son, it happened again! Mom has to tell you what happened last evening." So I picked up the bedroom phone and told the usual story how someone thought I was his dad's mother.

When I came to the part mimicking the female photographer, "O-oh you found yourself a boy-toy", our son immediately chuckled, but quickly interrupted (because he knows I am not currently updated). "Mom, I am telling you … that woman is watching way too much TV.

They call women who are marrying younger men, cougars."

Once again, I gasped, "You mean, like I am a predator?"

"Exactly!" he assured me.

I then assured him, "Well, I think it is about time to start calling boy-toy, your baby-faced dad, Junior Johnson, by his legal name, Wilfred Clarence Johnson Jr. That just sounds a lot older!"

Seriously, I am just having a whole lot of fun with you, the reader, by telling this true story because actually I like his young looks, while I don't mind looking my age. Giving my husband guff is just something I enjoy.

Besides, I know my husband absolutely adores me. In our many decades of marriage he has affectionately attached many nicknames to me. He has lovingly called me his Bobtail Queen (Bobtail is our street), Precious and Cupcake. But now, thanks to this professional photographer, he calls me his Cougar.

Oh well, as long as he keeps chasing, cuddling, complimenting and coming up with these adoring nicknames, I don't care if I am considered his cougar, his *Wild Wife!*

MAKING THE HONEYMOON LAST

A 10-year-old granddaughter asked, "How old are you, Grandma?"

Startled, Grandma replied, "Honey, at my age, you don't share that with anybody."

Grandma then got busy preparing supper, and before long realized her granddaughter had been absent for about 20 minutes. Checking, she found her upstairs in the bedroom. The child had dumped her grandmother's purse on top of her bed and was sitting in the middle of the mess, holding her grandmother's driver's license.

Junior & Margie, Kootenai Falls, July 10, 2016

"Grandma, you're 76!" the child announced.

"Why, yes, I am. How did you know that?"

"I found the date of your birthday here on your driver's license."

The little girl continued, staring at the driver's license, "You also made an 'F' in sex, Grandma!"

Sooner or later, every marriage suffers from some stagnant times. We occasionally lose the wind in our romantic sails. But, Montana women, no matter what one's age, no one wants to make an 'F' in sex! I will share how we can make that 'F' stand for flirt, and keep the romance present in our relationships.

I was reading how back in the wooden boat era, sailors feared many things: pirates, storms and diseases. But a sailor's greatest fear was his ship encountering the doldrums, an area in the ocean near the equator where wind shifts very little. With no wind in their sails, this could mean death for the crew. Often they'd drift for days ...even weeks. They feared their food and water supply being exhausted. Sailors caught in the doldrums were desperate for a breeze to put them back on course.

Marriages that were once exciting and loving can get caught in the romance doldrums, even bringing a slow and painful death to the relationship. Certainly no instant, magic fix is likely for a stagnant marriage. But we can begin by laying aside excuses and working creatively to revive our marriages.

Hebrews 13:4 says, "Let marriage be held in honor." Creating pleasure in a marriage shows that you esteem your marriage and believe it's worth working on and improving.

Proverbs 5:18 encourages rejoicing in our marriages. Notice what husbands are told in verse 19: "Let her affection fill you at all times with delight, be infatuated always with her love." Infatuation involves being inspired with foolish love or affection.

One evening my husband came home eager to inform me that he

had heard on the radio that a person burns nine calories in a kiss. Then after a couple of pumps of his eyebrows and a wide grin, be added, "But I'll bet I can get one that burns 30!" That is acting foolishly in love with affection.

Was your honeymoon the last time you remember acting foolishly in love with affection?

Honeymooners know how to have fun in marriage. They are free-spirited, appreciative, comical, playful, and even goofy at times, treating time together joyfully and of utmost importance.

We all started marriage that way. Sometime after becoming parents, we became too serious and stopped having fun. Often that's when couples stop their husband and wife role and start their mom and dad role. But children and grandchildren need to see how much we love each other.

While raising children, keeping our honeymoon happening is vital. Seeing Mommy and Daddy and Grandma and Grandpa in love fills a fundamental security God designed children to need. When we play in our marriages, that's when our children relax with us, relate with us, and want to be around us. Yes, even our teenagers!

A saying in Africa is "When two elephants fight, it's the grass that suffers." This means that when parents fight, the children are the ones who are hurt. Remember back when your parents fought? Your world came crashing in! But when your parents had fun together, you felt on top of the world. Or do you remember your parents having fun?

Here are some specific ways to create romantic fun, but first a word of caution: What works in my marriage may not work for you. My husband enjoys certain attention, like having the world for an audience. That same attention may embarrass your husband. So never do anything that would embarrass your mate, whereas my husband hasn't fully tamed his wild wife.

On the highway coming home, I posted six huge heart-shaped signs for my husband reading, "Junior Johnson, I can't wait for you to get home tonight!"

The next seven miles he read:
  "You're my hero!"
  "Can't you drive faster?"
  "Being married to you is marvelous!"
  "210 years of marriage wouldn't be enough!"
  "Wow! You're home!"

That last sign should have read, "Please, do not disturb!" because cars drove up our dirt road just to read it.

Here are some less public but equally effective ways to put some romance back in your marriage:

When packing your husband's lunch, put your ruby-red lipstick on and kiss the outside of his white bread. If you leave for work before he's awake, kiss the back of his hand, or write a romantic message with lipstick or soap on the bathroom mirror or his windshield. These things are great for our kids and grandkids to catch a glimpse of our flirty fun.

Don't wait for an anniversary. Set the entire family down for dinner and eat by candlelight occasionally. Serve the first meal you cooked after being married. Or make Dad's favorite dessert for no other reason than that he is special. Perhaps, even surprise him with a homemade card on which you write all the reasons why you married him.

Surprise your husband with a 'Mystery Tour'. Previously plan and prepay for a Dinner Cruise. Or select something you know he would especially enjoy, like a car museum or relaxing train ride. Maybe spend the night in Montana's Glacier National Park.

If there is no time or finances for getaways, make time for each other every day. Take a little time after the kids go to bed or even over a cup of coffee in the morning before work.

Save all your loose pocket change until you can splurge and do something memorable for your mate. I saved for five years for the following special Valentine's Day: (Again, remember this is a warning -

Junior has a wild wife.)

I phoned Junior and said the car had broken down and to please pick me up at a certain gift shop. When he arrived, I was gone. The owner said, handing him a small envelope, "Your wife bought you a Huckleberry milkshake, but you first have to read this card aloud." He smiled and read, "Want to be my valentine? You'll have to chase me! Come to Center Drug."

At the Center Drug, three clerks stood smiling with a gift, waving another tiny card. He read, "I know tomorrow's Valentine's Day, but you'll have to catch me today. Come immediately to the sporting goods store."

Walking in, Junior smiled, "I know, I need to read you guys a note!" They laughed and listened, "I love being chased by you! I know now you'd follow me to the ends of the earth. Grab your hefty gift certificate and meet me at Hallmark."

That small card directed him to our friend's house. There he read, "You've just about captured your flirting and fleeting Valentine. See your shaving kit and clothes? Bath and change quickly! I'm waiting at Venture Inn Restaurant. Your Valentine, (truly captured).

When he arrived, ours was the only table with a lace tablecloth, a beautiful rose, and flickering candle. Ladies, that's how you keep your husband chasing you!

Don't let your marriage drift into the doldrums. Don't get bogged down being parents and grandparents. Don't wait for your marriage to happen … make it happen! Get back to being a husband and wife. Keep your newly-wed spirit. Act as if you've been married only 10 minutes.

THOSE SAPPY EMPTY NESTERS

The couple, standing in the driveway, watched as their last child left for college. The wife tearfully turns to her husband and sobs, "You're all I have left."

The husband replied, "I'm all you had to start with!"

Seeing our last child leave the nest can be tough. But then again it can be tons of fun!

Speaking of that, remember that TV commercial where the couple was dabbing tears and waving goodbye to their last child leaving home? But once the child was out of sight, these empty nesters turned off their tears and rushed into the house. Feeling free again, they started dancing around the kitchen to blaring music from their "Rock and Roll" era and pulled out hidden junk food from the freezer. In the midst of all the loud music, hugging, dancing, eating and really "whooping it up," suddenly the doorbell rang. Everything came to a silent halt. Seriousness was written all over their faces as they answer the door. There stood their other child, loaded down with all his gear, ready to move back home. Remember that commercial?

Many Montana moms feel like either crying in the driveway or dancing in the kitchen. Or maybe they feel a little bit of both...empty and elated.

One of my best girlfriends, Jaynee Bernall (seen in the photo along with her husband Don) lives in Dillon, Montana where they are now empty nesters, and seemed to have the right words. She said that feeling sad and happy at the same time is called "feeling sappy!"

Whether single of married, working or not working, younger or older, we all need this healthy attitude. We are sad because we are learning to let go, yet happy because we are getting to go on. If you

Don and Jaynee Bernall

want this attitude, it just takes a balancing act in the head to make this sappy mindset work.

Here's how. Let's say the house now seems too quiet and one day you are extra weepy. You stop in the hallway to lovingly gaze at their baby photo. That hollowed-out heart of a mother in you wishes you had gotten them bronzed, instead of their baby shoes. But immediately balance that thought. If you had all boys like Jaynee and I did, you remember the reality. A sense of relief causes a smile to suddenly spread across your face as you remember ... no more rushing down this hallway, pinching my nose while hauling out smelly, moldy tennis shoes.

Or, let's say you are sadly sitting alone at the breakfast table eating your last child's leftover box of highly sugared cereal. Don't just sit there stirring soggy cereal. Look at the bright side! Jump up and rush to the grocery store and (not caring who sees you) in the middle of the cereal aisle yank down a winner's fist and yell, "Yes!" Because now you are free to buy cereal for the fiber and not some fun quiz on the back of the box.

Also boredom may raise its ugly head. When it does, pull out those projects you've placed on the top shelf. Be glad there will be no interruptions. Bring out all those future plans you've placed on life's back burner, whether sorting photos, volunteer work, taking a college course or finishing a quilt. Reinvent or redefine your life. Doing so is a gift from God.

Go spoil yourself. Do it guilt-free. Maybe now is the time to make an appointment for that glorious foot massage. Or go have an extra long lunch with that meaningful friend you've been wanting to catch up with. Some how change your sad mind into a glad mind.

Life as an empty nester can be exciting, but only if we don't wait for life to happen. Instead, make it happen! Remember that old saying, "Don't wait for your ship to come in, swim out and meet it."

Since I have been an empty nester, I've published 2 books and dozens of articles, traveled extensively, started public speaking, opened my own catering business and started my "Decorate on a Dime" business. Now I am working on my 3rd book!

None of this is said to brag, but to help you to believe. If I can do it, you can. And if you don't know how to swim to go meet your ship, then doggie-paddle, for goodness sake! I did.... the entire way! Seriously, I did not even know how to type, prepare a speech, plan a trip to a foreign country or track business expenses until I was in my forties. You just jump in and doggie-paddle toward your dreams, keeping your head above water and gasping a lot in between. Soon being an empty nester quits being a job and becomes a joy.

Empty nesters, your life now is like filling a book full of new chapters. So don't waste time. If finances don't fit or health doesn't permit, you can still expand your horizon. We can all afford to help others in some way or afford to experience travel through a book.

I'm reminded of the young, excited mother who just found out she was pregnant. Proudly cupping her tummy with both hands, she asked her middle-aged doctor, "When will my baby move?" He answered, "Hopefully right after he graduates!" We can all guess what was happening in that doctor's life.

Okay, so now my talking about our grown kids living at home isn't intended to step on anyone's toes, so hear me through. Being an empty nester is necessary. Nature itself teaches us our children are designed to leave the nest. How else do they learn to be responsible and fly on their own? Birds actually make it uncomfortable for the baby birds to stay in the nest. The mother bird places twigs that are poking up, making it tough for the babies to rest. You could say the chicks eventually get the point!

I shared this analogy one night in Idaho where I was speaking on A Woman's Life. When I came to the subject of the sad empty nester, I explained how an empty nest does not mean empty arms. Unlike the birds, ours do return to visit the empty nest. And then again, there may be the problem of a child returning and wanting to stay.

After my talk that evening, an older lady came up to me and shared, "When my brother got out of the army, he came home and stayed... and stayed...and stayed! Then one evening he came to the dinner table and there was no place set for him." She then winked, "I think my brother got the point."

Montana moms, I know there are exceptions. Sometimes our grown children need to return home to live temporarily. College debt, health problems, or helping a young married couple get their feet under them may all be god reasons. Bringing them back home to stay for a while may be understandable. But if we do, for their sake, we must sit down together and make a plan with a date attached for them to leave. And keep to that plan. If not, the birds would have a name for us…just plain sappy!

IS THE CAR REGISTRATION
SOMETHING I SHOULD HAVE WITH ME?

Are you married to one of those "one in a million" Montana men? All right, I know there are barely a million people in Montana, let alone men. But are you married to a rare guy? I am! He is not perfect, but you might confuse him for being that.

Let me back up. Sitting here on my front porch sipping my morning coffee and planning to clean my car today, a particular marriage memory concerning my car tumbled across my mind… a memory worth sharing, so here goes.

One day, flying down the highway in my suped-up, 1998 red Mustang, with loud pipes roaring and 1950s hot rod music blaring, here came those dreaded flashing lights, pulling me over. Doggone it!

Getting stopped for speeding was a first for me. Seriously, I am unfamiliar with the procedure. The officer asked to see my driver's

Wild Wife Margie, 1998 Mustang GT, September 14, 2013

license and car registration.

Now I am being even more serious with you. I innocently asked, "Is the car registration something I should have with me?"

He nodded toward my dash and suggested, "If you have one, it is probably in your glove compartment." Meanwhile, as I was digging, he reviewed my driver's license.

Paperwork has always been my husband's department in our marriage, so I was hoping he had put the car registration in there. And sure enough, digging deep, I found an envelope he'd boldly entitled "Car Registration". Not looking inside the envelope, I immediately handed it to the waiting officer. While he was reading it, I couldn't help noticing the smile that broke across his face. He handed it back with all the contents now outside the envelope. That is when I noticed a note from my husband on top of the registration. It read, "Honey, if you are reading this; either you got stopped or were in an accident. I just want you to know… it's, okay. I won't be mad. I am just glad you aren't hurt and able to read this. I love you, Junior."

See what I mean about being married to a guy who is "one in million"? I felt that hidden note was worth the price of the speeding ticket I was probably going to get. Because of the discovered love note I would think of the ticket as being handed a bouquet of flowers. To make a long story short, I didn't get ticketed. However, I was reprimanded and strictly warned to slow down.

Sitting here on my front porch sipping my coffee and enjoying the memory of my husband's past kindness and thoughtfulness, I still get all revved up! In fact, so much so I am not only going to clean my car today, but before he gets home I am going to fix his favorite dinner, freshly polish my 60-some year old toenails, put on a favorite outfit and then go meet him at his truck after work, hand him a frosted glass of Coke and give him a kiss that will last 10 glorious seconds! Lastly, I plan to somehow sneak a message on his truck's rearview mirror before he goes to work tomorrow morning that reads, "Looking back, 210 years with you won't be enough... love, your wild wife."

Why am I revved up to do all this even though that happened years earlier?

Two things: my deep appreciation for my husband lives endlessly in me and actually enlivens me. That leads to the second reason. I never wanted one of those marriages that exist in mediocrity. You know, staying alive the same humdrum way every day… eat breakfast, give a peck on the cheek good-bye, then stare at the evening news together before lying down, snoring and snorting in sequence like a full orchestrated symphony.

Yikes! I'd rather bust out and break the boredom. I continually find creative ways to chase my husband and compliment him for being such a rarity (or willing to be married to one). He is my hero. So, till my dying day I will appreciate him and bring out the best in him. God made me female and He gave me the power to have a great influence on my husband. As a Montana woman, I help to make him who he is, "one in million."

Just to confirm everything: after writing this I told my husband, "I just wrote about you."

He asked, "What is it about?"

I responded, "It's about you being one in a million."

He immediately shot back, "Shoot, that's you!"

What can I say? We are, after all these years, in the habit of always bringing out the best in each other. That is what God intended for a good marriage.

MY AMERICAN HERO

My husband and I were invited to attend "Dancing with the Stars and Stripes," a community ball in Helena, Montana. As I was clearing off my office desk this morning, this photo of that event popped up. So with photo in hand and cup of coffee in the other, (and forgetting my messy desk) I found my way outside and plopped in my front porch wicker chair to study my husband's face.

Have you ever looked long and hard at a photo and sensed what a certain person means to you? That's what I found myself doing. That's what I want to talk about.

My husband is my hero! Montana women, I hope you feel the same about yours. Now, I'm not saying your husband has had to be or is in the military to be your hero. In fact I am not even thinking saving lives, bravery, Superman, conqueror, champion or anything of the sort that we usually attach to being a hero. I want to go deeper, to the inner being of a man. He could be working at a fast food place or on disability and sitting in a wheel chair for the point I want to make.

My husband will not even know I wrote this until he picks up and reads this book.

What makes my husband my hero? His integrity - he is consciously honest and dependable. He has an extra deep sense of compassion for others. Along with that, he excels in remarkable qualities of kindness and gentleness and is long-suffering and patient. He is a Christian.

He is confident and never confused when needing to confront tough situations. He is able to quickly discern right and wrong. I admire such insight.

Mostly, I appreciate how naturally and easily he applauds and compliment others. He actually delights in other people's success.

Junior & Margie, 2007

Above that, he has the gift of wearing someone else's pain.

He is the type of guy you want on your side whether you have succeeded or failed. He cares to understand even when someone has caused their own hurt. In fact, the other night when I was going to bed, he was at the kitchen table writing someone in Montana State Prison. He wanted to give that person hope. He wanted him to believe there is a brighter side to every battle. Being optimistic is so-o-o him!

I guess that is why I see my husband as a ladder holder. He rejoices with those at the top, yet is willing to help those at the bottom.

I admire how he is satisfied just being who God created him to be. He is the same person around those who are successful as well as those who consider themselves failures.

He knows in a busy life when to say no and he knows how to say it politely.

He knows how to drop doing the important things to go do the urgent things.

He has the same temperament at 3 o'clock in the morning as 3 o'clock in the afternoon.

When I am sad, he knows how to reach in and string dainty lights around my broken heart. He knows how to go clothes shopping with me and patiently wait while I try on things. When I thank him, he says, "I enjoyed the style show."

Those are just a few of the reasons I look at this photo and see a hero.

Sipping my last drop of morning coffee and still sitting here looking deep into this photo, I still remember that first kiss. I knew it was terminal!

Parenting & Grandparenting

WHAT KIND OF PARENT
DO YOU WANT TO BE REMEMBERED FOR?

A father wanted his young son to learn geography, so he took a map of the world, ripped it up, and handing it to the little boy, said, "Go put this puzzle together."

The little boy quickly returned, handing his father the world all put together. Surprised, the father knew his young son couldn't have known how to do it so quickly, so he asked him, "How did you know to do this?"

The little boy turned the paper over and replied, "I knew if I got this little boy to turn out, then the whole world would."

Wow! Isn't that true? If we want the world to turn out or become a better place, then as parents we need to put our kids together properly.

Putting our kids together properly starts early. Toddlers are like little walking sponges, slurping up everything we say and do. And smart! By age two, they know every fault we have. By age three, they know how to exploit every fault we have. And by age four they are mimicking every fault we have!

So how does one put kids together properly? Many things are involved in raising responsible children, but consider two: First, start young in your children's lives. Mold them while you can hold them. This is not only your opportunity, it's your obligation. Billy Graham was right when he said, "We are the product of our earliest experiences." Many shocking articles and news segments are coming out now about how our schools and courts are filled with children who are lacking the instilled traits such as compassion, responsibility, honesty and respect for one another. That should scare us.

And that brings me to my second point: If you want to teach your children values and morals, then you need to be willing to be that example yourself.

One day in a Bible study a man read Proverb 22:6, "Train up a child in the way he should go, and when he is old he will not depart from it." Thinking a moment, he profoundly added, "Parents, maybe today that would be better understood if it read, '"Train up a child in the way he should go, but be willing to go that way yourself!"

My sister Shirley Kihs with her daughter Teresa Hall

We are not going to fool our kids. They are smarter than we think when it comes to preaching one thing, yet living another. Living a double standard is living a lie in front of them. Often we do it in ways that we don't think count or consider important. For instance, we warn them, "Don't lie." A few minutes later the telephone rings and we yell, "If that's for me, tell them I'm not home!" Or, "Don't cheat." Yet, they grow up riding in the family car with a radar-detector on the dash.

Perhaps we are driving with the family and imparting some wisdom on the virtue of being patient. About that time another driver pulls out in front of our car and we blurt, "What is wrong with that stupid fool? Can't he see?"

We tell our children, "You need to be responsible for your actions." But we're an exception to the rule and make all kinds of excuses for someone else making us angry at work. Or we want them to learn to be a person of integrity. Yet, we promise we are going to spend time with them in their favorite activity, knowing well we have no intentions of fulfilling that promise. It was only to get them off our back.

You get the idea. As parents, we have all been guilty of saying one thing, yet doing another. We need to stop living a double standard because our kids become who we are, not who we say we are.

However, to give some hope here, God did make our kids renewable!

When they see us mess up, but we then make a sincere apology to them, they respect us even more. Making that needed admission of guilt is often the time when we make ourselves not only real as parents, but safe as parents. When we allow ourselves to be transparent we are often doing our best parenting. We are transferring (trans-parenting) ourselves to them! And hopefully that is something good.

Shoveling away at our own egotistical pride is an unthreatening beginning to becoming a powerful parent. When we admit our own failures or weaknesses we allow them to see us as real. Parents, we need to live what we preach. We aren't going to fool our kids. They will hold us accountable.

While visiting my grown niece Teresa (my sister Shirley's daughter), she announced in the middle of a conversation, "My mom is my hero!" Her compliment about her mother rang like music to my ears. Teresa knew her mom wasn't perfect, but more importantly, she knew her mom was always looking for ways to be perfected - a willing heart to better herself. That's the quality Teresa loved, what made her proud and what made her mom her hero.

There are many Montana moms who are their kid's hero. These moms can relate to the famous Irene Mattox when she said, "When God gave me my children, instead of giving me handfuls of clay to mold, He gave me chunks of marble to chisel. But when I got through, I really had something!"

Josh McDowell and Dick Day in their book, HOW TO BE A HERO TO YOUR KIDS, said it best as the bottom line. "You can con a con, you can fool a fool, but you can't kid a kid." So, be real. Be willing to better yourself. Kids want to look up to and admire their parents. Let's solve the puzzle. Let's put our kids together properly. Leave a legacy. Our children are the only message we will send into a world we will never see.

FROM THE LIPS OF LI'L KIDS!

When little kids put their heads together they have life all figured out. Their innocence instantly amuses us and warms our hearts.

A 1st grade school teacher presented the first half of a well-known adage and asked her class to come up with the remainder. Listen to the wit and wisdom of 6-year olds. Their insight may surprise you.

A penny saved is … not much.

It's always darkest befor … daylight saving time.

You can lead a horse to water but … how?

Libby and Allie Michael, granddaughters of Kathy Myhre and great nieces of Margie's in Libby, MT

A miss is as good as a … Mr.

You can't teach an old dog new … math.

Where there's smoke, there's … pollution.

Two's company, three's … The Musketeers.

Children should be seen and not … spanked or grounded.

If at first you don't succeed … get new batteries.

When the blind lead the blind … get out of the way.

A bird in the hand … is going to poop on you.

Better late than … pregnant.

If we would only keep life simple and learn to spell like they do:

One little boy was asked if he knew how to spell farm. He quickly responded, "E-I-E-I-O!"

A sweet little girl was asked her name and she replied, "Lynn." Then she was asked, "Is it spelled L-y- double-n?" "No-o", she responded, rolling her eyes as if to say, "This is ridiculous!" "It's spelled Ly-n-n!"

At the gym, I was standing beside a little boy, Chris, who was just learning to sound out words. I overheard him when his little buddy came rushing up, wiggling back and forth and stepping from foot to foot, wanting to know quickly where the boy's bathroom was. Still zipping his pants, Chris assured his little buddy by pointing toward the girls' bathroom, "I just used it! It says Gorillas."

Weddings are so easily misunderstood. Listen to the lips of these little ones:

A grandmother overheard 5-year-old Christy "playing wedding." The vows went something like this: "You have the right to remain silent;

anything you say may be held against you. You may now kiss the bride."

After little Justin attended his first wedding, he inquired to his mother, "Why can a man marry sixteen women?" "Well, wherever did you hear that?" asked the amazed mother. "It was easy," the little boy replied. "All I had to do was add them up when the pastor said, 4 better, 4 worse, 4 richer, 4 poorer."

Medical terms are tricky for kids:

My son's kindergarten teacher told how the school nurse came in the classroom and asked the children to raise their hand if they had ever had the Chicken Pox. One little girl, who is normally very shy, got very excited, raised her hand and squealed out of turn, "I never had the Chicken Pox, but I got the Goose Bumps!!"

One little girl was at the doctor's office. The doctor put the stethoscope on her small chest and said, "Let's see if Barney lives in there." The little girl quickly corrected the doctor, "Barney doesn't live in my heart. Jesus does. Barney is on my under panties."

Nature can be a mystery for little tykes:

A father took his little daughter for a walk and they came across a water puddle with an oil sheen on its surface. The daughter cheered, "Oh look Daddy, a dead rainbow!"

When young Bobby opened up the old family Bible, something fell out. He picked it up and studied it closely. It was an old leaf from a tree that had been pressed between the pages. "Mama, look what I found," Bobby called out. "What do you have?" his mother asked. "Well, I think it is Adam's clothes."

Paul Harvey told about a family going to visit a farm. Their little girl had never seen anything on a farm. She went out looking at the sights and came running, saying, "Mommy, there is a big pig out there and there are six little pigs blowing her up."

Technology is everyday life to little kids:

One 5-year-old, sitting on the sofa beside her grandmother, bragged, "Grandma, I have learned to sing the books of the New Testament. Let me sing them for you." She began, "Matthew, Mark, Luke and John, Fax the letter to the Romans."

A mother was teaching her 3-year-old daughter the Lord's Prayer. For several evenings at bedtime she repeated it after her mother. One night the girl was ready to go solo. The mother proudly listened as her darling had each word correct until the very end, "Lead us not into temptation," she prayed, "but deliver us some e-mail. Amen."

Kids are forever listening and willing to improve.

One little boy was overheard reciting the Lord's Prayer, "And forgive us our trash passes as we forgive those who passed the trash against us."

And lastly Montana parents, please make sure your big lips say only what you want little lips around you to repeat!

A little girl's father always drove her to preschool, but one week he was out of town and Mom had to drive her. After a little while the little girl sat up, looking over the dashboard and all around and asked, "Where did all the STUPID IDIOTS go?" Mom said, "I think they only come out when Dad drives."

MONTANA MYSTERY MORNING

"Wake up sleepy heads! Grandma J and Papa J are taking you on a Montana Mystery Morning."

Sitting up and rubbing their tired little eyes and remembering they are waking up in Montana and not Arkansas, their slight southern draw inquired, "What is that?"

"Okay," I informed them, "just get your clothes on quickly and meet us in the car and we will explain."

Kids love surprises. So in no time, our eight- and nine-year-old grandsons came rushing out to climb in our car. Pulling out of the driveway, we explained that for the next few hours we were going to make them guess where we were taking them. And the big clue for the mystery was that every place or thing we did would start with the letter M.

Garden of Eaten on Bobtail Cut-off Road with grand boys Cody & Conner

So, our first clue to the Mystery Morning was where we planned to eat that started with the letter M.

"McDonald's!" they screamed.

And we praised, "You guys are tough to fool."

"Ya'll are easy to guess, Grandma J and Papa J," letting us know our compliment was somewhat droopy.

Perched upon McDonald's tall chairs with their legs swinging, ready to chomp into breakfast, Papa J interrupted, "Hold it boys! What do you need to take with your breakfast that starts with the letter M?" (Just for you readers … he convinced our grand boys from the time they were young that his daily vitamins are M&M's candies.)

"Oh, I get it," both blurted out in a chorus. "M&M's candies!" So Papa J pulled out his small brown package and poured us each a handful of colorful morsels to eat before breakfast.

Now, seeing this was going to get fun and not so easy, they hurriedly jumped down out of their chairs, excited about clues for the next mystery place to guess. Some places they guessed that morning, but most they couldn't.

Driving to the beautiful and wide Kootenia River that winds its way through our community, we knew a 'Message in a Bottle' was something they'd never done. Writing a short note with their names and our phone number, we stuffed the paper in the corked bottle and they flipped a

M&M's are what Junior taught our grand boys are his daily vitamins

quarter to see who could give it a fling in the rapid. (Later that afternoon, a fisherman phoned our boys to tell them he found their message.)

Our Montana Mystery Morning was cram packed, just like the kids love. We visited places like a Music store, where they also sell coins or Money. We let them select a folder and start a coin collection. After our local Museum, we stopped at Mac's Market for a drink before taking them to Mountainside Ministry Center where Upward Basketball is played in Libby. (They both play Upward Basket ball in Arkansas.)

By then it was time to do some Munching (an extra hard one to guess) and we took them to this wonderful place called Garden of Eatin'. They dug carrots, snapped peas, pinched off bell peppers, picked berries and loved the entire experience of all the goodies to take home to eat.

Lastly, pulling up to our garage, tuckered out, they guessed the one last thing we do every year before leaving for the airport. We Measure them on the garage door wood frame to show how much they've grown.

Montana women, that memory-making Montana Morning Mystery Tour with our grand boys, whom we get to see only twice a year, was as much fun for us as it was for them. With a little creativeness, you can do the same.

I don't know about you, but I have been blessed to be in some incredible cities and even countries with my grandkids, but nothing brings out my best and who I really am … I am about home!

Home in Montana. Home in a small rural place that embraces memories near to my heart. I need no huge amusement park for the day or inside heated pool to splash in. I find being splashed by water balloons in my front yard or bringing out the snowballs from the freezer this August that I saved just for them last winter is more fun, or taking them to the bakery to see how a loaf of bread is cut, or asking my bank or credit union if they could show them where all the money is kept. And those are just a few of the endless and unusual fun things we've done in our small community. Creative fun at my home in Montana is what I want to be remembered for.

Imagine what those of you across the state of Montana with farm animals, or lake homes, or ranches or living in the state capitol can come up with for making a memorable impact on your grandchildren.

So sitting out on my front porch this beautiful summer morning with paper and pen in hand, planning this month's visit with our grand boys, my toes just get to wiggling! I can hardly sit and wait. I have pages of ideas. We will never get to do them all.

Montana gals, if you have grandkids coming this year, or are blessed to have them living in your community, don't just wait for memories to happen. Instead, get up and get creative and make them happen.

It's been said, "Grandparenting is our last chance to grow up," so don't miss your grand childhood.

HOW TO BE A LONG-DISTANCE,
YET HANDS-ON GRANDMA

An elderly woman and her little grandson, whose face was sprinkled with bright freckles, spent the day at the zoo. Lots of children were waiting in line to get their cheeks painted by a local artist who was decorating them with tiger paws. "You've got so many freckles, there's no place to paint!" a girl in the line said to the little boy.

Embarrassed, the little boy dropped his head. His grandmother knelt down next to him. "I love your freckles. When I was a little girl I always wanted freckles," she said, while tracing her finger across the child's cheek. "Freckles are beautiful!"

The boy looked up, "Really?"

"Of course," said the grandmother. "Why, just name me one thing that's prettier than freckles."

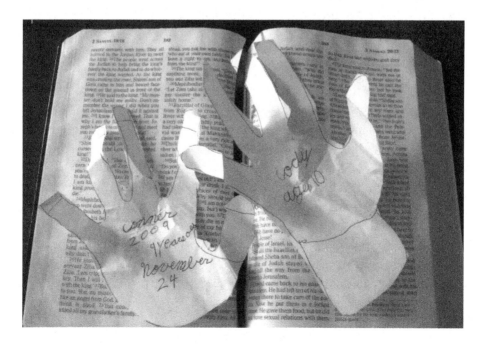

The little boy thought for a moment, peered intensely into his grandma's face, and softly whispered, "Wrinkles."

Montana grandmas, doesn't that story just make your heart melt?

Living in Montana, a big but very unpopulated state, causes many of us to do the 'long distance grandma thing'. We don't live close to our grandchildren and wanting to be a positive influence, we are always looking for ideas so we can be involved with them. Plus we need our 'Grandma fix'!

Even though we can't have physical contact like the grandma we just read about, we can find ways to help satisfy our nurturing souls. So here's a hands-on idea to help stay close in heart across the miles. This won't replace hugs, but certainly helps fulfill our need.

This past year I was in Arkansas visiting my two grandsons, Cody and Conner. I asked them to trace both their hands and cut them out. Being older and past doing those art projects, they wondered why. I explained, "Because Papa J and Grandma J (that's what they call us) will each place one of your hands in our Bible, and then every morning when we pray we will each hold your hand and pray for you." So, they very quickly handed me their paper hands project.

Once back home, I followed up by phoning and reminding them that every day we pray with them and for them. I even ask for their prayer request. Most often they struggle for something to suggest, but then at other times they are quite specific...especially if they want us to pray that they will win their upcoming tennis match! Obviously, that's what's important to them. So we do.

Now granted, clasping these worn out paper hands and praying for them may mean more to us as grandparents than it does to them. But it helps us believe in three things. One, that someday when they want prayers, they are comfortable to call and ask. Secondly, being a praying grandparent, we are leaving a legacy of our faith in God. And lastly, we will be satisfied or content in knowing our purpose may be more in prayer for them than our presence.

Meanwhile, I am sure glad that when we all get to heaven there is only one mansion to live in!

LONG-DISTANCE "GRANDMOTHERING"
HOW DO WE LIVE FAR AWAY IN MILES YET STAY CLOSE IN HEART?

I was snuggled between my two grandsons in the back seat while driving away from Kalispell, Montana's Glacier Park International Airport, and our oldest grandson Cody quit digging in the gift bag we had given him long enough to tap my shoulder and ask, "Why do you like me so much?" He said it with that "What's-in-it-for-you?" tone.

Conner & Cody Johnson

This simple question caused tears to puddle in the corners of my eyes. How could I help him grasp the beautiful and fulfilling meaning of my God-given role as grandmother? Although they brought new purpose to my life, little Cody was clueless as to why he deserved to be the center of my attention. And I was clueless to explain how once he and his brother Conner were born, they had immediate and intimate access to my heart.

But not everything is always beautiful and fulfilling about being their grandmother. I didn't know I would feel so empty-hearted and tearful when I became a long-distance grandmother. Thirty-six hours between us seems so unfair. While others' grandkids are just across the street, mine are across the United States. Negative feelings often nab me.

At school programs sometimes, others' grandkids are up front singing a song, and their grandparents beam with pride. But no little eyes search the audience looking for me. When with my friend, her grandchild's little fingers reach to find Gramma's; I have no warm little hand to hold in mine.

Many Montana women also suffer as long-distance grandmothers, and know what I'm talking about. We want to be positive influences, reinforcing Godly values and morals in their young lives. We want to offer time, security, acceptance and affection. Our deepest desire is being involved in their lives and being remembered by them. Our worst fear is being a stranger to them!

So how do we "barren" grandmothers make the best of not getting to grandmother like we would want? How do we live far away in miles yet stay close in heart?

HUGS ACROSS THE MILES

Missing my grand kids has caused me to become creative across the miles. Let me share some of the helpful hands-on hints I have discovered. They don't replace hugs, but they certainly help fill our void.

Praying for my grandchildren and "grand mothering" has taught me that my purpose may be more in prayer for them, not just my presence.

What is crucial next is being involved with them consistently by using the post office, telephone, computer, smart phone and texting. Start by sending your framed picture for their bedrooms. Updated photos keep them reminded of who you are.

When they are young, hang a play mailbox or basket on their bedroom wall. Get them in the habit of finding inexpensive gifts from you. Mail small items regularly, like stickers, gum, cookies or post cards. Teenagers enjoy $5 gift certificates from McDonalds or surprise pizza delivery. Any age likes photos reminding them of past good times together.

Send a gift of some sort every month. This needn't be expensive. The popular dollar stores have popped up everywhere. My grandsons like even weird things like dead bugs from Montana or unique rocks from our area.

Don't be discouraged by mailing costs. Think light weight when you buy, and that memories are worth the money. Sacrifice sipping that daily espresso. Instead, send a memory to your grandchildren.

Call the grandkids by a special nickname, if their parents don't mind. We call our grandsons "Major" and "Colonel." We tell them that's because they rank so high in our lives!

The telephone is another way to reach out and touch and be touched. When they were young, we would pay to hear them "ga-ga" and "goo-goo" over the phone. Then when they were older, we paid to blow train whistles or sing silly songs over the phone. I have even read their parents favorite childhood book over the phone.

Remind them on the phone of special memories you made together. Ask them about their favorite memories. Encourage them to share their goals and dreams.

Conner & Cody Johnson

Leave messages telling them you called because you needed your "Grandma Dose." Express how much you love, miss and think of them.

Specifically decorate for them a bedroom in your home, whatever their age. Because our grandsons live in Arkansas, we decorated a real "Montana Experience" bedroom for them with bears, fish, moose, etc. Put special sheets on their beds with favorite cartoon characters. When we talk on the phone, we refer to their bedroom and actually sit in there while we face-time on our phone. They often ask about their toys they remember on the shelves. They usually want us to blow their train whistle or play their drum. But you get the idea; phones connect and create real feelings.

Modern technology also shrinks the grandparent gap. Grandchildren love hearing stories about their parents when they were young. Text a funny story or joke to them. E-mail them "I Miss You" cards to make them feel special. Technology allows us to instantly share our job, travels and holidays which helps build our relationships. Ask them to show off their talent by reading to you, playing a musical instrument, playing sports or doing gymnastic routines.

Although long-distance grandparenting can be difficult, it need not be impossible. Be inventive. Your creative juices will begin to flow. You won't run out of bonding ideas. Just think, you may even cultivate more closeness than if they lived in the same town and you took them for granted!

The blessing of continually doing all these little things means every visit won't be an effort to get reacquainted. Instead, you use "away time" to cultivate a continuing closeness so that when you are together, your hearts are already entwined.

Sometimes, I still choose to whine and carry-on. But then I get creative and mail something unique. And when I do this, a bandage from above floats down and wraps around my broken heart. I then smile, thankful that I get to be a grandmother....even if it's across the miles. And when they come to see me, I make it a real "Montana experience!"

Grief

Grief Works

&

Funerals

MOST EMBARRASSING
BUT MEMORABLE MOOSE HUNT

Our five-year-old Kevin excitedly came rushing out of his bedroom with his toy rifle, shouting with his speech impediment, "Daddy takin' me moot huntin' and we willy gonna toot one!" (Kevin's R's and S's came later)

My husband Junior smiled and winked, informing me, "We're taking the Volkswagen bug moose hunting."

I understood taking "the bug" and his winking meant he was merely road-hunting by scouting out his designated area. He'd go back later with his pickup for the serious harvesting of his big game animal.

Kevin age 5

Junior applied for this special permit for years, so being selected was a dream come true. Many Montana hunters hungered for the same Moose Permit. So Junior answered plenty of phone calls wishing him well and wanting a return call when they could come and see his huge rack.

Not much later, puttering around in my kitchen, I looked out the window because I heard this long car beep in our driveway. Junior and Kevin were already back. Wearing humongous smiles, they proudly waved me to come outside. But more shocking was to see a moose stuffed in the backseat of our Volkswagen bug! Four gangly legs were stretching out every window past their ears and smiling faces.

Before Junior could give any details, Kevin, all hyped up and still experiencing that "hunters euphoria", started yelling (not telling) his version of the hunt. Enthused out of his skin, he furthermore started signaling people over. I mean he drew a small crowd out of the woodwork in this trailer park we lived in at the time.

It was bad enough all the neighbors witnessed Junior's yearling, but Kevin's story version only made his Daddy look worse. And because Kevin was jabbering so loud and fast, I remember actually being glad he had such a bad speech impediment, hoping no one could understand him. Obviously my poor husband, melting with embarrassment, interrupted, "No Son, let Daddy tell what ..."

But he couldn't counteract fueled-up Kevin who insisted, "No, Daddy, I taw ev'y tang."

I knew Junior had a good explanation for "the bug" hauling the moose. But he was being careful not to dishearten his proud little hunter, who continued misleading his audience by touching the moose's bleeding nose, informing, "My Daddy tot dis big moot wight 'ere. Then I telped 'tuff him in the back teat of the tar. We willy, willy had to work tard."

I looked pathetically, first to Junior and then his frowning jury. I knew they understood Kevin's every word of how his daddy shot this big moose in the nose and how hard it was to help stuff him in the back seat of the car.

Junior's flushed face quit attempting to correct Kevin's enthusiasm. So his dear daddy swallowed his pride and took another route of explanation before his wide-eyed onlookers by joking, "We could have waited and shot a bigger one, but because there was no milk on the lips, I decided this is guaranteed tender meat!"

Somewhere in the embarrassment of it all, everyone evaporated.

That evening after Kevin went to bed, still wearing that same smile, Junior recovered his blown ego. He shared with me the rest of the story, actually quite a heroic one.

For me to effectively tell this story, allow me to move you ahead to five years later. It was the second time I heard it. The atmosphere was quite sobering. Kevin was in Intensive Care.

Turning from the rain-spattered window, I walked over to sit and weep with Junior, a torn-hearted daddy. We had been waiting in Intensive Care all day. Our nine-year-old Kevin had had two cardiac arrests during what was to be a simple appendectomy.

Sitting beside my husband, I decided he was just as lonely as I, waiting and wondering what the outcome would be, although doctors had leveled with us that there was very little hope of Kevin surviving.

Leaning forward, Junior had his head bent down and his elbows on his knees. Watching him stare into the carpet, I wondered what he was thinking. I really wanted to know.

Reaching around his strong shoulders, I pressed my cheek tight to him. He looked over at me. He gave me a small, quivering smile. His Scandinavian blue eyes were red-rimmed. On the verge of crying, he faithfully patted my arm as he always does when he is emotionally touched. I asked, "Tell me what you are thinking?"

My small amount of comfort and wanting into his world made his sturdy shoulders droop and start shaking. He buried his whisker-stubbled face in his calloused diesel mechanic hands, spread wide over his forehead. I heard his sobs and felt the hurt that shot through him. I wanted to be there for him; so often in the past twenty-four hours he had held me and kissed my tears. Besides, at a time like this I didn't need a Superman. I needed a man who is sensitive and not afraid to show his hurt and can relate to my pain.

Therefore, I knew the relief he felt when he finished shedding what was like tons of weight from his shoulders. He sat up and tilted his head back, resting it on the wall. Then taking a few shaky, deep breaths, he let me know he'd not forgotten my question.

"I was just missing Kevin, thinking about that time I got that moose permit." Chuckling and half smiling to himself, he sniffled and went on, "Remember how many years I put in for that big game permit and waited to get one? And then when I finally did get it, I let that li'l guy stand there with his toy rifle and beg me into shooting one that wasn't much bigger than Bambie. Margie, you would not believe the excitement on his face that day. I only put the animal in my scope just for the fun. But when I looked down and tried to explain how the moose was too small, Kevin was trembling with excitement. He knew his toy rifle couldn't shoot it, so he started begging and pleading and asking me why. Then he began to cry and before I knew it, I did it because my heart got in the way. All I could think was, 'Man, if I was a li'l kid and my dad took me out like this, I would have never forgotten this!'"

Humored in his hurt, Junior went on, "I shot it in the lungs, but all Kevin could see was a bloody nose. And I know from where he stood down there, those long gangly legs made that moose look huge to him. And he was convinced of that when he helped lift and stuff those awkward legs in the backseat. Then coming home, he wanted to know if we could drive down the main street of town like all the other hunters do. And so I did. I did it for him."

Tears welled up in his eyes again, and his voice stumbled, breaking, "Honey, I'm glad more than ever now I shot that moose for him. I don't think I'll ever get that chance again. When I did it, I thought it was more for him someday to grow up and remember… but now I think the memory will be more for me."

And it was, because Kevin died and went to live with his Heavenly Father a few days later.

And every hunting season that rolls around, I'm still reminded how blessed I am to be married to such a caring Montana man and Kevin was to have him for a Montana daddy. One who could let go of his manly ego, in order to build up the pride in his little boy. He easily amplified the beautiful philosophy, "Life is not lost in dying. Life is lost in a thousand small, uncaring ways."

THE HARDEST / EASIEST THING I'VE EVER DONE

Many years ago, one April morning, my tears splashed down on our child's cold, expressionless face. Nine-year-old Kevin lay dying in Intensive Care from a reaction to the anesthesia during a simple appendectomy.

Kevin's downward spiral began Sunday. His heart stopped twice. Monday, he was flown to a major hospital. Tuesday, his kidneys started failing. By Wednesday, I wondered if I was embracing a corpse.

Waiting was difficult. Reading get well cards, watering flowers and walking to the hospital's cafeteria were all that could be done. Clocks and schedules were useless. My husband Junior and I told time by what the cafeteria was serving... cereal, sandwiches or potatoes and gravy.

Doctors broke up our long hours by consulting with us every time they tried something new. But they leveled with us; the prognosis was not good.

Wednesday night, Junior and I talked about how we would accept whatever God gave us to deal with. Turned toward each other, we clasped hands and took turns praying. Junior's words moved on his lips, near my hand. Having him for a prayer partner felt good. We cried, holding each other until the hurt ran off our shoulders, honoring us with some sleep.

Thursday morning, I walked in catching Kevin's nurse quickly turning away and wiping tears from her eyes. That told me that nothing parents, doctors, nurses or machines did would make what happened "unhappen".

This would be my hardest and easiest day, my letting-go day. Every griever needs a letting-go day to move forward in grief.

Being alone in the room with Kevin felt good, even familiar. At home, many nights found me sneaking into my sleeping boys' room and kneeling in prayer to thank God for giving me that day with them and to ask that I might use tomorrow wisely. Being here was almost like old times. But this time the prayer was not for Kevin's tomorrow, but for help in giving him up.

Finding the willingness to say goodbye and to give my child freely to God required my deepest trust. But if I could love Kevin so much, how much more could God love him? As long as our child was with

Travis 6, Kevin 4 - 1976

God and we kept near God, Kevin would never be far away.

Laying my hot, swollen face next to his cold, swollen face, I gave him physical warmth one last time, which hurt. Surveying his still, little form, I tried to forget the noisy machines and unfamiliar apparatus tangled around him, thinking instead about how he had once been - energized and exhausting.

My words were broken: "Goodbye, son. Mommy loves you. I'm going to miss you; Daddy, Brother Travis… we all are. This is a tough time to let you go. You were just growing into those front teeth, and your legs were even getting lanky. Remember the last time you sat on my lap? You were so big we had to exchange places. You really liked that. You started that obnoxious giggle until I scolded you. I'm going to miss that sort of stuff, too - always taking my patience to the limit.

"I don't know what I'm going to do, having it so quiet around the house. Probably some days I'll expect to see you come rushing out of your bedroom. But you won't. Your absence is going to leave a loud silence. Everything is going to take some getting used to. But we will. We will have to."

Turning from my goodbye to Kevin, I turned to God and said my shortest, yet deepest prayer. "Help me, dear Lord. Please just help me to live apart from him until I see him again someday."

I felt no regrets, selfishness nor unfairness. Only a deep trust lay between me and God.

Walking backwards out of the room, humility and trust accompanied me to the door. Strangely enough, I even felt dignity. With no strings attached, God had helped me give back to Him this valuable little treasure He had entrusted to me for such a short time.

I freely handed Kevin back, carefully polished and as beautiful as the day God lent him to me. I had done a good job as a mother, although it hurt to think my job was done.

Walking to the waiting room I almost felt guilt. Adoring and trusting God at a time like this could be easily misunderstood. Some people might believe I didn't love my child. Already, some people misunderstood my hope. They confused it for lack of my being in touch with reality. But God knew I understood heaven is true reality.

The next day at noon on Good Friday, Kevin died. Machines were unplugged. Kevin completed his earthly life and was ushered with nobility and grandeur into the next.

Being Christians, we chose to understand only one thing from then on. Heaven had always been our ultimate goal for Kevin. Our child had made it to heaven, the greater life's beautiful entrance.

Many years now have passed since that Easter time when our child died on Good Friday. Yet never does a year pass that my husband and I don't rinse ourselves in the reminding pain of letting go.

This past Christmas Day morning, we phoned our surviving son

Travis at his home in Arkansas. It was his birthday. While wishing him a Happy Birthday and Merry Christmas, I eagerly added, "Son, God must think we are special parents!"

He asked, "Why is that?"

Loving to answer him, I replied, "Because He gave us you on Jesus' birthday and He took Kevin home on the day of Jesus' death."

"Hmm," he quickly agreed. "That's a good way to think of it!"

Many of you too, have lost children. You had plans and dreams of how you wanted life to turn out for them, but suddenly losing them left a huge hole in your heart that you learn to live around.

The other day a friend, Jo Neils, and I were talking about raising our children as Christians and she made this profound statement. "Our children are just on loan from God. He wants them back with interest in Him."

What Jo shared struck me. Being a mother and losing my child was the hardest thing I've ever done. Yet, what made it become the easiest thing I've ever done was accepting that I could do nothing but unselfishly let go and trust in all that I'd taught him about his home in heaven.

Along with that, while raising Kevin I understood he was a gift on loan to me for a little while. The Lord was gracious enough to design me to conceive and care for Kevin, but He always wanted me to understand I had not created him! My role was as his mother, not his Maker. Accepting this difference was essential.

So, accepting the difference made the hardest thing I've ever done become the easiest thing I've ever done. That is how I define having faith.

I WILL NEVER FORGET

April isn't my easiest month. A gnawing pain, as though new, nibbles away at my already tattered heart as I remember back to that April when our nine-year-old son Kevin passed away unexpectedly from what was to be a routine appendectomy nearly 40 years ago.

There's a saying, "People who are in pain are our teachers." That is true. I found in my early grief, by listening to other grieving parents who had years behind them, that losing a child does not mean they have to be forgotten. (The fear of loved ones being forgotten is important to grievers. I know it's confusing how the fear of forgetting and the pain of remembering both struggle to reside in the same grieving heart. That is just part of grief's complexity.)

The following grievers were my teachers. I actually wrote their stories down back in my early grief of losing Kevin.

One early spring afternoon I visited with a lady in her eighties who was proudly telling me, in depth, about her several children in the order of their ages, what they do and where they live. Suddenly she stopped to tell me that one had died over fifty years ago. Tears filled her frail eyes. She took her dainty handkerchief with its embroidered edges and dabbed at the evidence of pain spilling over. I knew grief was still there, even after all these years. Before being able to continue on to tell me about her next child, her weak voice trembled, "I still remember him like it was yesterday."

That eighty-year-old lady's fifty-year-old sorrow encouraged me. Her deceased son was still remembered. Unforgotten. He will always be mentioned in her line of children and honored in her heavy heart.

I experienced this same feeling of recent emptiness from another mother who shared losing her little girl twenty-some years previously to a disease. She was still hungry after all those years to talk about that daughter. When she did, she started out clear, but soon her voice broke. It was obvious the importance of her past pain was still a part of her as much as a thorn belongs to a delicate rose.

A third person who taught me the grief of losing a child will last all your life, was actually a tough looking, Montana man.

After Kevin died, I went to work a couple of days a week in a small clothing store. One day was an unusually quiet business day, one of those when you have time to visit with

Kevin 9 - 1981

customers. A sturdy man who looked to be mid-fifties walked in. There were only the two of us and somehow we got on the subject of children. I did not know the man, but in the short time he was paying for his new Western belt buckle, he poured out his heart... and I will never forget him. Standing at the counter, pain twisted his face; it became so distorted he seemed to age thirty years! His shoulders went into a slump as he reminisced how his son (and only child) was killed in a car accident as he followed him home late one evening. Tears began tumbling down the stubble on his face, spreading into his deep creases. I remember thinking then that because he was a man he would quit talking at any time. But he didn't. He continued expressing his limitless pain for his son after the many years of his loss. And by then his tears overflowed the crevices and started spattering on the counter, forming a puddle in front of us. He didn't wipe them away. I did after he left.

And I was glad too. In fact, I was humbled to wipe up this man's tears. If there had been a way, I would have bottled them up and returned them, thanking him for teaching me that crying is God's way of distilling or purifying our hearts. I wanted to let him know he reminded me of the Bible verse saying our tears are treated as a beautiful keepsake. "You have collected all my tears and preserved them in your bottle!" Psalms 56:8

Yes, in my pain other grievers have taught me that my son Kevin will always be meaningful to me as painful as it is remembering him. I will never have to worry I will forget him. Not next April or centuries of Aprils from now.

No, I will never forget Kevin. Not as long as mothers name their little boys Kevin. Whenever I hear the name, I will think of my little Kevin, and emptiness will run through me. Some days I even say his name. When I do, he sounds so long ago. Other days I say his name, and he sounds only a few minutes old. I can so easily have everything back: his voice, his exhausting energy, his teasing nature, his trusting eyes, his angelic smile, his silly problems and his chimpanzee hugs. I can have everything, but him.

I will never forget him. Not as long as I walk into his old bedroom. The décor is different and his closet is empty. The only thing that hasn't changed is my memories.

I will never forget him. Not as long as I wake up in the stillness of the night after dreaming about him. My memories are awakened. I can lie there still feeling his bare, little bony shoulders that I used to hug. But when morning light comes I get up and learn to live with what I don't have.

I will never forget him. Not as long as I see his now grown-up friends who have graduated, married and holding the hands of their own children. I can't keep from wondering… Would Kevin be that tall? Would his hair still be light blonde? What would he have done after graduation? What kind of girl would he have married? Would he have had children? I will never know. But I will never forget him.

I never want to forget Kevin. Remembering him is all I have left. My remembering him is my lasting grief.

It is said that a child who dies has a way of belonging to us more than our other children who live. Our living children are taken away by school, job, marriage, friends and other commitments in life but the child who dies remains tucked away in the depths of our heart. Life doesn't demand them anymore, so they can belong to us forever.

HELPING THE HURTING
WHAT CAN I SAY?

Every 30 seconds an American family suffers a death. As caring human beings we can serve those who are grief-stricken and help ease their pain by following some simple do's and don'ts.

• Most important is to go. Being fearful or worrying about what we will say is actually selfishness because we are concentrating more on our needs than griever's needs.

• Greet the bereaved with a hug. Touch feels good to tense shoulders. When our 9-year-son died, supportive embraces felt good, clinging to me like warm wax melting over the sides of a candle.

• Should the person want to talk, find a quiet place. A ringing telephone, buzzing doorbell, blaring television or fussing baby make effective listening nearly impossible. Get the griever alone even if this requires sitting in the bathroom or on the basement steps. Taking the initiative and finding a place with no distractions shows you think what the griever has to say is very important.

• Use non-verbal communication. Sit with a posture that says, "I'm here for you" and "I care about what you are feeling right now." Maintain eye contact. Looking away, sitting in a slothful position, and twitching indicate you would rather be somewhere else. Body language may be silent, but speaks loudly.

• Some grievers may want to talk but need help to start expressing their feelings. Give them an opening by expressing yours first. No eloquent speech is necessary. Simply say, "I am very sorry to hear about your loss." But remember that you are there to be a listener; after showing concern, center your attention on what the bereaved wants to express. Be all ears and little tongue.

• Be a keen listener. Hear when grievers do not want to talk. Pay attention to their reactions. Their not adding anything to your comments may mean they do not want to talk right then. Perhaps a troubled sigh is saying, "It's too hard to talk." Totally changing the subject to something like, "How is your family doing?" may be their way of saying, "I don't want to talk about me and my pain right now." Good listeners need the insight to read signals.

• Let grievers express feelings honestly. While one may voice anger at God, another may extol appreciation for Jesus' death and a hope in His all-important coming again. Either way, let them express without feeling judgment from you.

• Let the griever talk about the person who has died. They may want to share personal experiences. Let them relate memories. Relate some of your own favorite memories of the one who died. This sharing is comforting and reassuring that their loved ones' life was not in vain.

• Be honest. Admit, "Although I cannot fully comprehend what you must be experiencing, I am here for you." Those were the words of my dear friend Edie, who had never experienced the loss of a child but honestly sympathized with my loss.

• Avoid being a changer. Continually changing feet, messing with pocket change, or changing the subject are insults. You may be in pain listening, but bear it without shuffling.

• Do not expect recent grievers to be good listeners. Bombarded with thoughts of their deceased, they will probably not hear you. Concentration becomes poor. They easily forget everything you expressed, which is another reason you need not be overly worried about what you will say.

• Do not compare your or anyone else's grief with theirs. Especially do not bother them with your current pressing problems, whether it is paying your property tax or your neighbor's noisy dog keeping you awake at night…no matter how great they may seem at the moment. Trivial complaints will only irritate them, not interest them or distract them. Do not forget, you are there to listen, not be listened to.

• Absolutely do not protect or try helping them along in their sorrow by saying such things as, "You'll get over this in time" or "Life goes on." The bereaved will end all communication with you if you in any way minimize their hurt. They will feel as if you are belittling something immensely important to them.

• Another absolute is not judging the fate of the deceased. Your friend may be in your estimation, overly or even lacking in confidence in a loved one's salvation. Assure them of God's great love for His creation then drop the subject. God is to judge. We are there to listen, not to evaluate.

• Do not break a confidence. Grievers may share some deep secret from their heart about their deceased loved one. Wanting to get rid of some guilt, they may share something very intimate. Do not repeat it. Being a good listener means being faithful. Do not betray their trust. (Proverbs 20:19)

• Visit more than once. Go again and again during their early grief. Keep your visits short, only five to ten minutes long. Longer visits will be appreciated more later on.

These suggestions will help you successfully lend a listening ear to believers and non-believers alike. Remember, do not worry about what you are going to say. Your value is not in words of wisdom, but in what they feel from your presence.

FAMILY FEUDS AT THE FUNERAL

He wanted buried in a pine box, just a simple funeral. Nothing fancy! His single life as a missionary, seeing hunger and devastation, made him desire no luxuries. So the grief-stricken siblings fulfilled their brother's deathbed wish.

At the cemetery when the pine box was being lowered in the ground, a distressed sister panicked, "Turn it around! His head's at the other end."

"No!" the scowling siblings corrected her, pointing, "His head's at this end." But the distressed sister insisted.

Finally, to save onlookers from an embarrassing family feud, the siblings relented. The adamant sister got her way. But more than that, she got them so mad they haven't spoken to her since.

Another friend, dabbing teary eyes, shared her family feud: Her voice angrily quaked with disgust over her mother. "When our daughter died, I was taking her picture down off the wall for the funeral and my Mother calmly stated, 'Oh, she had such beautiful blue eyes.'"

"I was so angry at her! She had brown eyes, not blue!! I'll never forgive her for that! She didn't even know her own granddaughter!"

That poor grandmother's simple goof-up caused her daughter to erupt like a dragon spitting fire. (Understand, when a grandchild dies, grandparents get "double whammies". They hurt for both their child and grandchild. Besides, age makes us all forgetful.)

One grieving teenage girl shared her mother's knife stabbing remark. "When my sister died, my mother screamed at me, 'Why couldn't it have been you who died? Your sister's the one who got the good grades and had the promising future!'"

Maybe you know or belong to a family who has been feuding since the funeral. Relatives can actually refuse to speak for years!

Maybe some selfish family member yanked mementos that rightfully weren't theirs. Maybe your only childhood photos are tucked away in some cousin's closet. Maybe, being an only daughter, your Mother's wedding ring is being worn by a brother's stepdaughter. Maybe your grandmother's quilt promised to you is hanging in some ex-sister-in-law's and new husband's apartment. How could you not but feel unfairness?

Maybe it's not souvenirs separating siblings, but disagreeing on the burial place or preacher. Maybe it's collecting funeral expenses from family. Even distributing money can disrupt relationships! Maybe a sister provided health care, but she felt her inheritance never covered the cost as caretaker.

Then we all have those touchy relatives who get their dander up over simple things - like being the last one contacted about the death. Or they pout because no one asked their preference of flowers. Or their name was mistakenly left off the obituary, but they suspect it was intentional. Anyway, it's annoying dealing with touchy relatives who walk around like a porcupine with ingrown quills.

Speaking of touchy, maybe it's us, the immediate griever. We are stressed and easily nudged, making more out of a statement that's innocently intended. After losing our nine-year-old son, I was talking to an acquaintance in Texas, who also lost her child. She shared, "After my daughter's funeral, a relative was admiring a bouquet and had the nerve to say, "'I'm sure glad she died while these Chrysanthemums were in bloom!'"

Certainly, I didn't laugh, but inside it struck me funny. Probably, feeling awkward, her relative simply meant how beautiful the flowers were this time of year.

Grievers need to be careful. We can get hung up on the words and miss the love that someone is trying express. It's tough talking to us as grievers. We need to make certain we don't make it any tougher, and even more importantly, that our heart isn't in the wrong place. Perhaps, because of some long ago, unrelated problem with a certain relative, we think now we can justify our past anger.

But aside from crazy comments, for the most part, money, wills, personal items and religion are the causes of bitter disputes. Thoughtless comments and "piddley" problems usually wear off if ignored, but it's those bitter disputes that live for generations leaving relatives not speaking for decades. The details of their disagreement differ, depending on who's telling the story. But when two opinionated family members bicker, extended families are easily caught in the crossfire. Standing on the outside, they're soon driven to take sides and forever live like relatives of the Hatfields and McCoys.

Point is: Once a family feud is left to fester, it takes on a life of its own.

So, how can we stop generations of family feuds from festering?

If scripture teaches, "A friend loves at all times," then certainly there's no reduced responsibility for family to love at all times. Family should be our best friends.

Stabbing, abusive remarks made by parents to their child, like we read above, may require immediate Christian counseling. But for the most part, patience, understanding and sometime sacrificing dissolves discord when dealing with difficult relatives.

First, it helps to understand what causes family tension when grieving. Grievers are usually governed by their hearts rather than their heads. So when charged emotions rule instead of supervised thinking, things get touchy. Before long, impatience breeds unintended quarrels and tension snaps like a stretched rubber band. Verbal attacks are made. Deadly venom starts spurting out, ruining relationships. Often pride prevents apologies and that becomes the problem.

Contributing also to this stress is sleep loss and diet change, like tipping too much caffeine and nibbling sugary treats. Not to mention needing to make major decisions in too little time, because funerals are here and gone.

Quickly, how do we heal past family feuds? Sometimes pride becomes so permanent it's nearly impossible. But try! Start by trying to establish some common ground. Write a brief, newsy note. Wait for a response. If nothing, try later. Sadly, sometimes relationships can't be salvaged. But some are simply by saying, "I want to make a fresh new start."

How do we avoid future family feuds?

When uncalled for statements are blurted out, try understanding what happened from the other person's perspective. This takes submission. Maybe we can't control another's tongue, but we can control ours. In the same vein, don't try interpreting relatives' thoughtless, irritating remarks. It's best to give them the benefit of the doubt. Peace melts over us when we believe others are out for our best interest.

Keep yourself from being caught up in family crossfire. Be responsible. Stay out. Instead, attempt peacemaking.

What about serious issues like money, wills, religion or personal items? Certainly, seek what's rightfully yours, even having an opinion. But should selfishness surface, step aside. Lift that person in prayer to God. Maturing sometimes requires even a greater growth than submitting. It's the willingness to sacrifice.

Remember that missionary whose headstone became his footstone? What did it really matter? When resurrected, I'm sure God knows us from head to foot.

But speaking of headstones, I read what one lady had engraved on hers - that highway sign that reads, END OF CONSTRUCTION. THANK - YOU FOR YOUR PATIENCE

Maybe that's what we all need posted. Aren't we all under construction requiring God's patience? Why retaliate or hold a grudge with a relative at the time of a loved one's death? Keeping wrongs will keep us weary. Besides, we already have enough to grieve over.

WHAT DO YOU WANT YOUR HEADSTONE TO SAY?

Sometimes my late night mind runs rampant. Strange thoughts pop into my head-- like what do I want written on my headstone. Maybe you also find your late night mind flashes with unusual thoughts that normally never occur to you during the day.

However, I need to be careful not to agree fully that headstones aren't in my thoughts during the day, because through the years I've collected a few funny epitaphs. Entertaining inscriptions have always tickled my interest. Their witty words often tell us something the deceased person wants us to remember about them. But more often, I believe family and friends decide what they want said about us. And that may not be so good! Maybe we should write our own. You will see why.

First, I want to acknowledge my appreciation for all those veterans who gave their life and fought for America's freedom and never returned. In respect of them, my heart salutes them. Also, by my sharing a few humorous headstones, regardless of what they say, please know I value each and every grave inscribed to a beloved father, mother, son, daughter, sister or brother.

Epitaphs vary from being military formal to everyday informal or even downright funny! We all know people who want to be remembered for living on the lighter side of life. Some want to take their witty personality to the grave with them. Or again, someone else wants to cleverly do it for them.

For example: One in an old northwest cemetery reads,
"Here lies the body of old man Peas buried beneath the flowers and trees. But Peas ain't here, just the pod. Peas shelled-out and went to God."

This one is a little confusing. I figured it was written by a first-time-poet-of-a-husband who, in his grief, is a little disgusted, yet reluctant to let go of his wife, and maybe even a tad bit glad all at the same time.

"Here lays the body of Samantha Proctor. She 'catched' a cold and wouldn't doctor. She couldn't stay. She had to go. Praise God from whom all blessings flow."

This man evidently felt mad and neglected. His headstone read, "See, I told you I was sick!"

On a tombstone over a hundred years old, this departed soul stops us in our steps, sounding somewhat eerie, like a ghost from the past, demanding… "Pause, stranger, when you pass me by. As you are now, so once was I. As I am now, so you will be. Prepare yourself to follow me."

Some brave person came along and wrote a note beneath: "To follow you, I'm not content until I know which way you went."

Well, that does it! That just goes to prove, even if we write our own epitaph, there is no guarantee we will have the last word.

SPECIAL DELIVERY FOR MOTHER'S DAY

Mom,

I just wanted to take time out of my day and tell you how much I love you. Thank you so much for supporting Charele and me in all we do. I wish we could spend more time together, but distance keeps us apart. The boys are looking forward to coming up this summer to Montana and seeing their bedroom you decorated especially for them.

I hope you have a wonderful Mother's Day and again, thank you for being such a blessing in my life.

Love,
Travis

Travis emailed that card to me for Mother's Day. That alone was very touching, but to my surprise, he included the following special delivery Mother's Day card as though it had come from his little brother in heaven.

Mom,

It's been awhile since I have written but I am having so much fun up here in heaven. I can't wait until you see this place!

I want you to know that I love you dearly and could not have been more blessed to have you take care of me on Earth. You and Dad are always on my mind and I look so forward to holding you in my arms again someday. My nine years on Earth were short but the eternity we will spend together will never end.

I love you from the bottom of my heart and want to wish you a Happy Mother's Day.

Love,
Kevin

Montana Moms, it has been said, "Life is not measured by the number of breaths we take, but by the moments that take our breath away." So may your children's thoughtfulness also leave you speechless every Mother's Day.

Margie and Travis, Seaside, Florida - November 4, 2014

History

&

Education

SLEEPING WITH SMOKEY BEAR

Have you ever been hugged by Smokey Bear? This wild wife has. In fact recently ... tonight in the back woods of Montana! And tomorrow when he wakes up, he is going to wrap those big furry arms around smiling children who rush off the school bus to greet him for the first time. But for now he is snoring so loud he's lifting the roof off our house, making it impossible for me to go back to sleep. So, being as I'm wide-eyed and getting madder by the moment, I might as well get up and let him continue to snore and snort and smile and dream about his big upcoming day that the Forest Service invited him for. He's the mascot for education on wildfire prevention. I think I will go research how this hugging bear happen to originate.

Smokey's beginnings took place during a raging wildfire that ended up taking 17,000 acres in 1950 in Lincoln National Forest, in the Capitan Mountains of New Mexico. Here is how his story unfolds.

In a lookout, an operator spotted smoke and called the nearest ranger station. The first crew arrived and found a major fire being driven by wind, rapidly sweeping along the forest floor between trees. And just as rapidly, word spread, requiring more crews to help. Forest rangers, men from New Mexico State Game Department, Native American crews, army soldiers and civilian volunteers came to the aid. Teaming together to gain control of the raging flames still proved to be difficult. As soon as one hot spot was contained to one area, the relentless wind would whip flames across the barrier or fire-line. That is where firefighters reported seeing a lonely black bear cub wandering around. The crews left him alone, for fear the mother bear might be nearby and come for him.

On May 9th, 30 firefighters became even more endangered while fighting the fierce roar. They found themselves caught in the direct path of the firestorm. Laying face down on a rockslide for over an hour until the fire had burned past them saved their lives. They scarcely escaped, having only minor injuries.

That small cub seen wandering around earlier however, was caught in the same path and did not prosper as well. Taking refuge, he fled up a tree. When the firefighters removed the little 5-pound black bundle from the completely charred tree, they could see he was badly burned on the paws and hind legs. Not knowing what to do with him, a man who was a rancher helping the firefighters offered to take the orphaned cub home. And at that time the men named him "Hotfoot Teddy." Later he was renamed Smokey.

Wild Wife getting hugged by Smokey Bear, April 23, 2014

Hearing about the cub being rescued and in a safe place, a New Mexico Department of Game and Fish ranger drove to the rancher's home and saw that the cub needed veterinary aid. They flew him in a small plane to Santa Fe and his burns were treated and bandaged and he was nursed back to health.

By now the story of little "Hotfoot Teddy" surviving the wildfires had drawn national attention. That's the beginnings of his becoming a celebrity.

After recuperating, Hotfoot Teddy was flown via an aircraft called a Piper Cub to his final destination, the National Zoo in Washington D.C., which would become his home. However, due to a fuel stop during the trip, he had an overnight layover in a special room prepared for him at the St. Louis Zoo.

But upon arrival in Washington D.C., (and now being known as

Smokey) this celebrity had a greeting committee consisting of hundreds of fans. Nearby photographers snapped cameras, Boys Scouts and Girl Scouts jumped for joy, along with many other spectators lined up, waving and welcoming him to his new home.

Life for Smokey at the zoo for the next 26 years was extremely nice. After surviving such a raging forest fire, he was set up with what I would call "spoiling comforts." He had his pool to splash and play in. He loved lunching on peanut butter sandwiches. And on a daily bases he enjoyed bluefish and trout for dinner.

Smokey Bear fans poured in over the millions to view him. He received fan mail, bringing in up to 13,000 letters a week. So many, that in 1964 the United States Postal Service gave him his very own zip code.

During those 26 years, he had a family. He married "Goldie" in 1962. "Goldie" was an orphaned female black bear also from New Mexico. Unfortunately, unable to have any offspring, in 1971 the couple adopted a son, Little Smokey. He was also an orphaned cub from New Mexico.

On May 2, 1975, Smokey Bear formally "retired" from his leading position as a living mascot. His adopted son assumed the title, "Smokey Bear II". On November 9, 1976, Smokey died. The government had his remains returned to Capitan, New Mexico and he was buried at Smokey Bear Historical Park. One can read the plaque at his gravesite, "This is the resting place of the first living Smokey Bear...the living symbol of wildfire prevention and wildlife conservation."

Smokey will always be a living legend. Growing up, many of us remember all those posters of Smokey as an advertising mascot. He was created to educate the public about the dangers of wildfires. He was always depicted wearing his Forest Ranger hat with his name across the band and cuffed-up denim blue jeans with a big leather belt with a brass buckle.

Most of all, he was created to make a meaningful and influential impact. For instance, remember Smokey standing with the shovel in one hand and with his other hand's index finger pointing strictly in your face saying "ONLY YOU"? This is the image that children and families all across the United States recognized instantly, knowing exactly what Smokey's message was by his famous face alone.

And yet even though Smokey's advertising campaign goal was to create him to be simple, strong and straightforward, there was a gentler and polite side of Smokey's character depicted on posters. He was always proud of the Boy Scouts of America and the Camp Fire Girls. Posing behind them in their decorated uniforms, he challenged us with the words, "THEY HELP...DO YOU? Please Prevent Forest Fires!"

Whoa! I have never been involved as an animal advocate, but many of you are, therefore I know this story must profoundly touch you as it did me. My respect goes to the United States Forest Service and the Smokey Bear campaign, the cub who started it all and the people who healed and cared for him. Smokey's face and message are still vital in teaching kids the importance of fire safety and protecting our forests and wildlife.

Earlier I was wanting to clobber this big brute of a mascot who was raising the roof with his snoring. Instead, now I appreciate his purpose in being there to hug those important busloads of children tomorrow. In fact I am feeling so appreciative, I think I will wake up early and hand him his favorite cup of coffee, which he loves with a teaspoon of honey swirled in. Then I am going to wink when he sees me flipping his favorite... Montana huckleberry pancakes! Speaking of winks, I better go catch a few.

TOMB OF THE UNKNOWN SOLDIER

There are many Montana moms who are homeschoolers. I was not one myself, but both our grandsons, who live in another state, went all twelve years being homeschooled and are now attending college. A big advantage of their being taught at home was that our son and his wife encouraged good grades by promising instead of just reading about these certain places, they would actually visit them! The Tomb of the Unknown Soldier was just one of those countless trips. And as grandparents, we were often invited to go on these learning tours. And being a writer, I wanted to bring every Montana homeschooling mom this beneficial and interesting information.

So enjoy this quiz and educate your children with these 6 short questions.

1. How many steps does the guard take during his walk across the tomb of the Unknown Soldier and why?

Answer: 21 steps, alluding to the twenty-one-gun salute, which is the highest honor given any military dignitary.

2. How long does he hesitate after his about face to begin his return walk and why?

Answer: 21 seconds for the same reason as answer number 1.

3. Why are his gloves wet?

Answer: His gloves are moistened to prevent his losing his grip on the rifle.

4. Does he carry his rifle on the same shoulder all the time? And if not, why not?

Tomb of the Unknown Soldier - photo by ESGR

Answer: He carries the rifle on the shoulder away from the tomb. After his march across the path, he executes an about-face and moves the rifle to the outside shoulder.

5. How often are the guards changed?

Answer: Guards are changed every thirty minutes, twenty-four hours a day 365 days a year.

6. What are the physical traits of the guard limited to?

Answer: For a person to apply for guard duty at the Tomb he must be between 5'10" and 6'2" tall and his waist cannot exceed 30".

Other requirements of the Guard: They must commit two years of life to guard the Tomb, live in a barracks under the Tomb, and cannot drink any alcohol on or off duty for the rest of their lives. They cannot swear in public for the rest of their lives and cannot disgrace the uniform (fighting) or the Tomb in any way.

After two years, guards are given a wreath pin that is worn on their lapel signifying they served as guard of the Tomb. There are only 400 presently worn. The guards must obey these rules for the rest of their lives or give up the wreath pin.

The shoes are specially made with very thick soles to keep the heat and cold from their feet. There are metal heel plates that extend to the top of the shoe in order to make the loud click as they come to a halt.

There are no wrinkles, folds or lint on the uniform. Guards dress for duty in front of a full-length mirror.

During the first six months of duty, a guard cannot talk to anyone, nor watch TV. All off-duty time is spent studying the 175 notable people laid to rest in Arlington National Cemetery. A guard must memorize who they are and where they are interred. Among the notables are: President Taft, the boxer and Medal of Honor winner Joe E Lewis, and Audie Murphy, (the most decorated soldier of WWII) of Hollywood fame.

Every guard spends five hours a day getting his uniform ready for guard duty.

And just as an added note of interest:

In 2003 as Hurricane Isabelle was approaching Washington D.C., our U.S. Senate/House took 2 days off in anticipation of the storm. On ABC evening news it was reported that because of the dangers from the hurricane, the military members assigned the duty of guarding the Tomb of the Unknown Soldier were given permission to suspend the assignment. They respectively declined the offer, "No way, Sir!" Soaked to the skin, marching in the pelting rain of a tropical storm, they said that guarding the Tomb was not just an assignment; it was the highest honor that can be afforded to a service person. The Tomb has been patrolled continuously 24/7, since 1930.

YOUR NAME IS MUD!

Have you ever wondered where the saying, "Your name is mud" originated? Learning the stories behind old expressions fascinates me.

Junior & Margie with grandsons, Conner & Cody

While on tour in Washington, D.C. for ten days with our son and his family, here is the story as we learned it, behind the age-old, negative expression.

My husband is an Abraham Lincoln history enthusiast. So upon arriving in D.C., his first request was to fulfill his life-long dream of spending uninterrupted time in Ford's Theater, where Abraham Lincoln was assassinated April 14, 1865. And that is the beginning of the uncomplimentary expression, "Your name is mud!"

The four-year Civil War was drawing to an end and five days earlier, on April 9, 1865, General Robert E. Lee surrendered to Union General Ulysses S. Grant. President Lincoln had lost twenty pounds and, regardless of his haggard face, glowed with a festive spirit. He rode down the streets of Washington where flags were waving on his way to Ford's Theater for a well deserved evening of relaxation. In fact, it was marked on every church calendar as Good Friday. Yet, it was one that didn't turn out so well.

While the President sat in the "State Box" flanked by two American flags, enjoying the comedy, Tom Taylor's "Our American Cousin", the rebellious John Wilkes Booth was carrying out his plot to kill the President.

The President's assassination was part of a larger conspiracy to rally the Confederate troops to continue fighting. Sympathetic to the South, Booth was a part of that conspiracy. He was a 26-year-old exceedingly handsome, successful actor who was often on stage at Ford's Theater where he had access to the back stage.

That evening, John Wilkes Booth arrived at Ford's theater at around 10:15. He was dressed for riding a horse. He had also been drinking heavily. Because of his familiarity with the theater, he knew how to strategically access the second door leading into the "State Box". The President's to-be assassinator also likely knew the exact point in the comedy that the audience of more than 1,000 would roar with laughter, muffling the sound of a gunshot, and when they would least expect the following event:

Abruptly, Booth pushed open the door into the Presidential box and

Junior across from the Presidential box where Lincoln was shot by Booth

deliberately fired a .44 caliber Derringer, single-shot, muzzle-loading pocket pistol at the back of Lincoln's head. The President slumped forward in his chair. Booth, standing with a smoking pistol in one hand and a hunting knife in the other, was immediately involved in a scuffle with Major Rathbone in the box.

Booth savagely slashed the officer across the arm with his knife and broke loose and vaulted from the box. His quick leap of eleven feet from the railing and onto the stage would have been nothing for the actor, except that one of his spurs caught in a third flag that was draped below the box. This caused Booth to land off balance, breaking the small bone in his left leg. He hobbled rapidly across the stage. Once out the theater's back door, Booth quickly mounted and spurred his mare, making his getaway. From there the manhunt was on!

Booth met a second rider, co-conspirator David Herold, outside Washington and at about 4 a.m. the next morning, Booth and Herold were loudly rapping on the door of 32-year-old Dr. Samuel Mudd.

Mudd placed Booth in the guest room and treated his leg. The theory is that Booth paid Dr. Mudd $25 for two revolvers and a short-barreled rifle, along with getting directions to a trail to the nearby Zekiah Swamp. Then, approximately 12 hours later, Booth and Herold were off.

During the week after Lincoln's death, detectives visited Dr. Mudd's house several times. They were suspicious of Mudd because he was also a Southern sympathizer. Booth had been a guest in his home at least twice the previous fall, staying overnight on one occasion. On December 23rd they were seen together in Washington. However, Dr. Mudd later swore that when Booth came to his house he did not recognize him for he was wearing a shawl and false beard. However, a boot with John Wilkes Booth's name inside was found in his home. That evidence along with discrepancies in Dr. Mudd's story resulted in him being escorted to Old Capitol Prison.

A short time later, Booth and Herold were surrounded while hiding in a barn. Herold surrendered to the 16th New York Calvary, while Booth chose to stay in the barn that was set on fire.

Ultimately, eight individuals were charged with conspiracy in the Lincoln murder. At the trial of Booth's accomplices, four were hanged and four were imprisoned. Dr. Samuel Mudd was one of those imprisoned for life.

Passed down for generations, it is popularly believed that the saying, "Your name is mud," originated in bitterness because it was Mudd who set the broken leg of Lincoln's assassin, John Wilkes Booth.

Concluding with a note of interest: It is said Dr. Mudd was sentenced to life in prison (though, strictly speaking, he was abiding by his professional code of ethics) for helping an assassin. However, he later gained recognition for his tremendous contribution of working with patients during an outbreak of typhoid in the prison. In appreciation, President Andrew Johnson pardoned him in 1869.

WHAT A WEEKEND!
FLYING MONTANA'S BIG SKY

My husband spent over 26 years in the Montana Army National Guard. We both volunteered for ESGR (Employee Support of the Guard and Reserve). Now, what made my ESGR weekend so spectacular?

Not being a risk taker, I found myself in a difficult spot. I had this once-in-a-lifetime opportunity to fly with the Montana Air National Guard out of Great Falls in a KC 135R on a refueling mission for six fighter jets or F-16's.

Now relate with me. Have you ever been scared to do something new, yet more scared not to? You're afraid to go, yet more afraid of missing an opportunity? Then you know my tough spot. But I went.

We flew at 25,000 feet at approximately 400 MPH. Now I don't mind flying. In fact, I fly quite often. But knowing the mission is to refuel 6 fighter jets, and realizing all the fuel is in the tummy of our plane, and if the puzzle pieces don't match like you see in the photo ... this could be a big explosion. And I might add...that's one Big Bang Theory I believe in!

F-16 Refueling, Great Falls, Montana

It's exhilarating to lie down on your belly in the tail end of a huge cargo plane and watch an F-16 jet smoothly position underneath for refueling.

96

It's enthralling! Unexplainable excitement rushed through every cell in my body. (By the way, did I mention there are no frills on KC 135's? Military cargo planes are like the inside of a house with no sheetrock, with all the wire and plumbing exposed.)

What a spectacular experience I had in our beautiful Montana skies as we flew from Great Falls to Yellowstone Park. My fear dissipated. It always does when we quit focusing on self. Knowing patriotic men and women serve in our armed forces made my fear become nil. Our service men and women are able to place their fear in the right realm... an unwavering commitment to the mission of protecting our country's freedom.

After our exciting experience in the refueling mission, we were ushered into the cockpit. Still even more pride swelled inside me. Alongside, six fighter jets swarmed around us like yellow jackets. With thumbs-up, their pilots let us know it was a successful refueling mission.

I felt refueled myself. Never before had I been so proud to be an American! What an experience to feel such pride for every young man and woman who has, who is, and who will serve our country in this

KC-135, Great Falls, Montana

great nation of America. Thank you!

And to think fear almost stopped this most meaningful moment in my life.

Montana Cowboys

COWBOYS HAVE A LOT IN COMMON,
INCLUDING COMMON SENSE

Being a Montana woman who has never ridden a horse is beyond me. I never even married one! In fact you can easily pick my husband out in the photo. Cowboys have their very own natural pose and wear western garb - clothes like vests, shirts with pearly buttons and yokes across the shoulders, cowboy hats with big dimpled tops, cowboy boots and blue jeans with belts and big buckles.

When taking this photo, I encouraged my husband to place his hand in his pocket like he was ready to draw a gun from his hip like the real cowboys on both sides of him were doing. They laughed and, being a good sport, my husband sorta smiled... so my camera went "click."

Also, being a good sport, my un-cowboy husband was willing to ride horseback into Spanish Peaks Primitive Area, down by Bozeman, Montana, to elk hunt with these experienced riders. He had never hunted horseback before. In previous years, he'd shot five elk but he

from left - Jim Ward, Junior, Jim Gardner

did the walking and the packing, instead of the horse. His two amigos assured him this hunting trip would be a different adventure.

Making a long story short, they all came home empty-handed, as can happen sometimes with all experienced hunters. My husband however, enjoyed himself immensely with his good friends, Jim Ward from Bozeman, Montana on the left and the late Jim Garner from Libby, Montana on the far right.

Here's even more on how cowboys are a breed all of their own. Aside from their unique western attire and how they have a certain pose for a photo, they also have a lingo that's all their own. Their expressions or sayings are quite entertaining when giving wisdom or advice in how to stay out of trouble or else reap the repercussions. For example, "Don't squat with your spurs on!"

Cowboys have common sense. In fact recently, in my daily Bible reading, I stumbled upon Proverbs 3:21-23 and it refers to how common sense will "Keep you safe from defeat and disaster and from stumbling off the trail." Every cowboy out there should like how that verse reads from "The Living Bible" version.

I always thought common sense was God-given, meaning everyone is born with it, knowing what is right and what is wrong. But many people have corrected me. They say some people don't learn even after they have been beaten up by stupidity. A cowboy would simply put it… "You can't fix stupid!"

Following are what one might call cowboys proverbs that I've collected through the years. Thanks to cowboy Dan Murray from Libby, Montana handing me the book From Savvy Sayin's by Ken Alstad, I've added even more to my collection. Thanks Dan for your addition. It helps me appreciate even more of your cowboy culture.

Enjoy these nuggets of truth:

"Never slap a man who's chewing tobacco."

"Never kick a cow chip on a hot dry day."

"The quickest way to double your money is to fold it and put it back into your pocket."

"If you fall in the cactus patch, you kin expect to pick stickers."

"Never approach a bull from the front, a horse from the rear or a fool from any direction."

"A sure cure for a toothache is to tickle a mule's heel."

"It's hard to put a foot in a shut mouth."

"Admire a big horse. Saddle a small one."

"A man don't have thoughts about women till he's 35. Afore then, all he's got is feelings."

"A man who ain't got ideas of his own should be mighty careful who he borrows 'em from."

"Having a jealous wife means if you come home with a hair on your coat, you'd better have the horse to match."

"Nobody but cattle know why they stampede and they ain't talkin'. "

"An over-polite man is hidin' some mighty unpolite ideas."

"Sometimes you'll find a heap of thread on a mighty small spool."

"A saloon keeper loves a drunk, but not as a son-in-law."

"You can't measure water with a sieve."

"The West is famous for rare and wonderful sights. But the rarest of all is clean socks in a bunkhouse."

"Love your enemies but keep your gun oiled."

"Secrets are easy to hear and hard to keep."

"Shallow rivers and shallow minds freeze first."

"A good friend is one who tells you your faults in secret."

"Before you go into a canyon, know how you will get out."

"You can educate a fool, but you can't make him think."

"Some men are so stingy, they'd skin a flea for the hide and tallow."

"You can't be hurt by words you don't say."

"Never trust a guy who agrees with you. He's probably wrong."

"Sweat never drowned no-one."

"A man don't get thirsty till he can't get water."

"The teepee ain't been built that'll hold two families peaceably."

"Some men wouldn't know a cactus if they sat on one."

"Some men think the sun came up just to hear them crow."

"A blind horse kin see just as well from either end."

"A string around the finger helps you remember. A rope around your neck helps you forget."

"If you have a hill to climb, waitin' won't make it smaller."

"They say, 'The only place some people make a name for themselves is on a tombstone.' "

"Broke is what happens when you let your yearnin's get ahead of your earnin's."

"There ain't no way to practice gettin' hung."

"When a hypochondriac has measles, he tells you how many."

"A man who looks for easy work goes to bed tired."

Hope you enjoyed these sayings, as much as I did.

EVEN JOHN WAYNE
WON'T MESS WITH MONTANA WOMEN

Have you ever had one of those "wise guys" in your life who is just good at outsmarting you? Ya know, they leave you speechless? Because you're not as fast on the draw with words, they shoot you down and they're gone, kind of how John Wayne was in his Old Western movies. He always had the best last word. His self-assurance wasn't to be argued with; what he said was the law.

Well, my girlfriend's husband Don is sort of like that. He watched way too many John Wayne movies. But I got Don back good!

Here's what happened… I phoned his wife Elaine and after we chatted about a zillion small things like girlfriends do, I hung-up. Suddenly I remembered I forgot to mention why I had phoned in the first place. So immediately phoning back and knowing it was dinnertime, her husband, the "wise-guy" who likes to give me a bad time, answered the phone.

Very abruptly he answered, "Hello!"

I stated, "I'm sorry, but I meant to ask Elaine something. So let me quickly talk to her." And just as quickly to cover my tracks, I added, "And I know it's dinnertime… but give me a break and just get over it. Besides, what are you going to do about it?" (This guy has a way of encouraging you to act as tough as him.)

And exactly like him, he smartly asked, "What am I going to do about it?" I could imagine his face smirking as he answered, "Here's what I am going to do"… and he hung the phone up!

Left standing there stunned, holding a dead phone in my hand, only one word came to mind. In fact, I found myself loudly remarking "Audacity!" I thought, "The nerve of that man to hang up on me!"
Immediately, the wild woman in me started searched for ideas.

Junior & Margie at John Wayne Airport, California, February 26, 2013

Somehow I was going to get even with him for hanging up the phone on me.

Because my husband Junior is nice and I am normal, I waited until he left home for the evening. (My type of wild fun revenge would be a little too risky for him to enjoy.)

About 9 o'clock, when I knew my girlfriend had gone to bed for her very early morning shift, I made my mischievous phone call. Understand, this couple had their property up for sale.

R-r-ring. "Hello!" Again, I heard his abrupt cowboy voice, just like I wanted.

Putting on my best oriental accent, I spoke in a high pitch, "Yes, I come to Montana, America to buy your property, Mr. Key."

He immediately asked, "Who are you calling?"

"Mr. Key, you have your house and property for my horse …you sell me?"

"Y-yeah, but my name isn't Mr. Key!" he corrected.

"Mr. Key I come to Montana, America and I have lots of money to buy your home. And you have room for my horse on property."

"Yeah, I do. But I am not Mr. Key! Where are you from?" he inquired.

I started to repeat, "I come to Montana, Amer…."

"Yeah, yeah I know!" He interrupted. "I'm asking… what country are you from?"

Thinking quickly (and for whatever reason), I popped up with, "I come from Vietnam."

Then still trying to correct me, he assured, "Yeah, I have my home for sale and property for your horse, but my name isn't Mr. Key."

Acting then a little impatient, I persisted, " Okay, what is your first name?"

"What is my first name?" he loudly repeated.

"Yeah, Mr. Key what is your first name?"

"Don!" he gladly bolted back.

"Yeah," I assured him, "You are who I want to talk to … Donkey! Hee-haw! Hee-haw!" And I slammed down the phone!

Oh, I can't tell you how good this Montana wild woman felt! In fact, even though I was home alone, I went around jumping and jabbing my fists in the air like I had just won the gold medal in the World Olympics in a game called "Outsmarting Your Opponent." I was yelling, "Yes! Yes! I got him … I got him back good and he better never mess with women who live in Montana, America!"

Crime & Protection

CRIME: REDUCE YOUR RISK

The escalation of crime in communities today is frightening for women, especially if they are single or widowed.

After work one afternoon, my 32-year-old niece drove into her garage. Leaving her keys in the ignition, she stepped out of her car, clicked the garage door closed, and dragged herself upstairs to take a short nap before preparing dinner.

She woke suddenly to the rumbling sound of her car engine starting. Running downstairs, she opened the door to the garage, only to find it empty.

A week went by before police found her car in the woods. It was trashed, and her keys were gone. In addition, she also had left in the car some billing statements with her credit card numbers on them and social security number.

How did the thieves enter the garage? She had left the side door of the garage unlocked.

What can one do to lessen the chances of being affected by crime? Our grandmothers used the old adage, "An ounce of prevention is worth a pound of cure." Prevention can also help us avoid a great deal of worry.

Living in Montana and tucked many miles out in the woods away from neighbors, or traveling our Big Sky State on the open plains alone with no cell service, requires learning protective measures.

We all know such common sense preventions as locking windows and doors and leaving lights on, but you may find some of these additional hints fresh and informative. Certainly none of these ideas are foolproof, but they can greatly improve the odds.

First, learn a lesson from my niece. Do not leave your keys in the car, even at home in the garage. Also, never leave banking information, credit card billing statements, or anything with credit card or social security number in your car.

Never open the door to a stranger. Instead, slide a window open so the person can hear you. If they will also be able to see you and you have a shotgun, make sure they will see that, too.

Sleep with your car keys next to the bed on your nightstand. If you suspect some unwanted person is outside your home, hit your panic button. They won't stay around with that noise.

If an intruder is outside your door at night, just the loud cocking sound of an unloaded shotgun is undeniable. The intruder will not know the gun is not loaded, but will know the warning sound of danger.

Outside your front door on a hook, hang a man's extra large coat and a pair of size 14 boots. That would make one stop and think.

When leaving your home, place a $20 bill on the kitchen table. Every time you come home, before you go in and close the door, look through a window if possible or at least from the open doorway, to see if the money is still there. If it is not in its place, do not go inside.

Never leave notes on your door about being gone or when you will return. This is as good as an engraved invitation to thieves.

Very few burglars will enter a home when they believe people are at home. Should you confront a burglar however, the rule is to stay out of the way. Never stand between a burglar and the exit, and never try to stop him from leaving.

Have your car or house key in hand before reaching the door. When leaving your car to be serviced or parked, leave only your ignition key.

While shopping, be aware of your surroundings. Walk confidently. Make brief eye contact with approaching strangers.

If being attacked, never scream "Help!" People usually avoid getting involved. Always scream "Fire!" Everyone is curious to come to a fire.

Blow a whistle. It is not something they will turn around and use on you. The shrilling sound also may deter them from wanting to stay around you.

Obviously, carrying a cell phone is always a plus when in a predicament. However, your cell phone could be out of range, especially in certain areas of Montana. Carry a man's cap under the front seat of your vehicle and a rolled up ready-made sign the reads, "CALL POLICE" in the event you experience car trouble and are stranded. Then, make certain your doors are locked, tuck your hair underneath the cap and place your sign in the back rear window.

At no point should you roll down the window or step outside your vehicle. Never be talked into getting into a stranger's vehicle. Heed the old saying "If in doubt, don't do it!" Listen to those red-flag feelings that warn you. They may be God-given.

Travel with all luggage hidden in the car trunk. That includes hanging clothes. This announces you are traveling alone and that you are easy prey.

Leave enough space to pull around the vehicle in front of you when stopped at a traffic light or stop sign. If anyone approaches your vehicle in a threatening manner, pull away immediately.

Wearing expensive jewelry may be welcoming advertisement to a mugger. Turn you rings around so the stones are not visible.

To prevent purse snatching, use a front waist pack. Better yet, carry cash and credit cards in a front pocket or in an under-the-shirt pouch. This prevents pick-pocketing.

Do not enter an elevator with anyone if you feel uncomfortable. If someone suspicious steps into the elevator you occupy by yourself, get off. If you are in an elevator with another person, stand near the alarm and as many control buttons as possible.

112

Leaving a radio or television on in your home or hotel room when stepping out may inhibit an invader.

When parking at the mall, avoid parking next to a van. Assailants can yank you inside and be gone instantly.

When returning to your car, look underneath it from a distance. Attackers have been known to hide and slash the tendons above both heels, disabling their victims. Always have your car keys ready. And check the backseat before entering your car.

These helpful suggestions may better prepare you to avoid becoming some criminal's success story. Watchfulness can prevent worry!

$ $ Money

"WELL, WE GOTTA KEEP SOME MONEY, YA KNOW!"

One payday, my husband Junior asked me to cash our paycheck at the bank. He specifically wanted it in small bills.

That evening after dinner, he called our small boys Travis and Kevin to the kitchen table. He told them to count the money and call him back when they were finished.

They were young, but they thought they knew how to count that far. They did not, but they came up with an amount. It did not matter. My husband just wanted them to have a feel for the wad of money.

Sitting down, Junior asked the boys to give him what belonged to The Lord. Enthusiastically, all four of their hands slid over a good, healthy amount.

Junior frowned, repeating his question a little more clearly: "Boys, give me what belongs to The Lord." Again, but now a little less enthusiastically, they slid over another big pile, leaving only a small amount in front of themselves.

Frowning deeper, Junior said, "Boys, you aren't listening!" Daddy wants you to give him what belongs to God."

Now, downright disgusted, Travis shoved out his chubby hand and slid over the rest of the money, complaining, "Well, we gotta keep some for house and food ya know!" Of course Kevin joined in like any good lawyer would.

Pleased with the entire amount in front of him, Junior purposely ignored their comments. Instead, he praised them, making his point. "That's right, boys. It all belongs to God. But now watch closely."

He separated the money into two piles, one smaller and one larger.

"Look how little our Lord requires in comparison to how much He blesses us with so we can buy groceries and have a nice home."

Junior asked the boys to get their Bibles. Setting Kevin and Travis on his lap, Junior took their little fingers and pointed to these words, which he read aloud: "But seek first his kingdom and his righteousness, and all these things shall be yours as well." (Matthew 6:33 RSV)

Try this with your children and grandchildren. Teach them at an early age that everything is a blessing from God. Because He owns

Travis age 5, Kevin age 3

everything, He deserves what is first and not what is left when we get our paychecks.

The earlier we reverse our children's thinking about ownership, the easier they will accept it. We know because we were married with two children and had the difficult chore of reversing our own views!

INTEGRITY IN BECOMING DEBT FREE

Debt free! Boy, aren't those enticing words these days? At least they should be with the tsunami of money being poured into bailing out companies, banks and mortgages.

Speaking of a tsunami, being bombarded with debt can make one feel flooded or overwhelmed - like being in so deep and not know how to swim out.

It is said, "A drowning man does not complain about the size of the life preserver." So, seek professional help from a financial manager if drowning in debt. However, my encouragement is for those still swimming, those who can make it to shore by making a serious effort to start living within their means. In other words, when we have only X amount of dollars, we better not be buying Y and Z.

Besides, living within our means shows integrity. Haven't we all heard a whining "woe is me" attitude; how "Life is against me. I can hardly feed my family. We can't afford a nicer home, let alone a vacation." Yet, they probably never will as long as they eat out every night or order pizza in so they can enjoy their big screen TV with surround sound that doesn't fit in their undersized living room. Plus, they may be paying off a DUI and still engaging in a half-dozen more daily bad behaviors. Some people just prove laziness and poverty are first cousins.

Having integrity about our debt is claiming responsibility for signing a promissory note and then paying that debtor before satisfying our desire for instant gratification.

Again, there are always exceptions and people who aren't being irresponsible. For instance, some accident, family death, unfortunate divorce, job loss or health issue arose. But most can make an immense difference in monthly debt load by sticking to a budget with strict boundaries.

Personally, in our marriage, and being a family of four, we endured several shut downs, a couple of lay-offs, two job losses, along with hospitalization and a funeral for our child. My husband, a blue-collar worker, and I, a homemaker, decided in the beginning of our marriage to live on only his paycheck. That may not be popular today, but for us it may still be a priority and therefore, I genuinely believe for many it is still possible (which is a topic for another time). But my point is: Montana women, it was during the tough times that I learned to decorate, dress and dine on a dime. Tough financial times are when one's character is constructed. We pay for what we promised and buy only what we can afford. God honors lives with integrity. (Proverbs 11:6)

Here are common sense actions to take toward financial freedom:

No more eating away from home. Pack a sack lunch. Enjoying fast food places should be a crime in our conscience when spending money eating out and our doctor bill is overdue.

Don't step out window shopping. Once we pull that store door open and sense that attitude of 'I deserve', trouble is brewing. Instead, stay focused on becoming debt free. Financial freedom unloads a mountain of stress so we can truly enjoy life. That's what we really deserve!

No more spoiling ourselves with professional manicures and pedicures. Montana gals, no one loves staying feminine more than I do… bar none! But this scene absolutely blows my mind. How does one charmingly walk out of the nail salon to her car in her cute little flip-flops sporting a palm tree on her dainty big toe, then press it to the pedal while admiring her new acrylic nails as she drives past the place of business where her house or vehicle payment is way overdue? Does that require sleepwalking or what? Toes and fingers can still be pretty with the stroke of our own polish and press-on palm tree.

No more exercising at the gym when the electric company is threatening to shut off the switch. Find a free way to exercise. (I didn't say freeway.)

While grocery shopping, pass by bargains that are not a part of our healthy food groups. Believe me, gals, instead of fatter bellies and flatter budgets, we will have flatter bellies and fatter budgets.

One day, I ran into a couple that was in a tough situation and whom we were personally helping financially. But after sharing with my husband, we changed our minds about desiring to support them any longer because of their lack of scruples. Here's what happened:

Wheeling my grocery cart, I ran into this seemingly under-privileged couple. Seriously, they were literally loading their cart with candy. They excitedly chatted about finding their family's favorite treats at half price.

Again, we all know people like that. Most likely, their finances will never get fixed. Stopping our support that was enabling this behavior was the right choice. The next time I saw them in the store, they walked over sucking lattes, carrying two flats of frosted donuts and showed us the paperbacks they love to read. Impulse buying is something even debt free people are cautious about. You'd think those impoverished would do the same.

You get the idea. Many of you could tell similar stories about those on limited budgets, behind in paying bills and spending money on items they don't need. Our integrity should come before our self-indulgence: pay our bills before buying personal wants. There are just some things we must deny ourselves if we want to swim out of debt.

Becoming debt free requires mental scrutiny. We intellectually examine every item we consider purchasing, whether to wear, eat, drive, repair, enjoy, etc. We honestly place that item mentally in one of two categories: needs or wants.

Disciplined, we purchase only our needs. For instance, potatoes can be a need, but potatoes chips are always a want. Water to drink is a need, but bottled water is not (as long as your tap water is safe). A doctor's office visit is probably a need, seldom a want. A dependable work vehicle is a need, while a new one is a want. Chocolate syrup to lawn furniture to breast implants to tattoos are wants, while a working refrigerator is a need. You get the idea… don't buy just anything you want. Buy only what you absolutely need.

I'm not suggesting we need to become such miserly Montana women or so frugal that we resort to reusing our aluminum foil. But if debtors were pounding on my door or phoning my home, undoubtedly I'd scrub, fold and save it!

Furthermore, in order to maintain integrity by rightly paying debtors, it is probably best to sell unnecessary items like recreational vehicles, big screen TV's, expensive furniture, jewelry, electronics, as well as cancel extra cell phones, satellite TV etc. Many may feel that selling purchased items or denying themselves a shiny new vehicle is stooping too low. Their self-image is way too important. Perhaps they think integrity is something outward rather than inward.

What is it worth to us to live debt free? Is it worth stooping and selling things like our diamonds or designer purses or dream home that shows our dignified position?

The good news is that probably everything we give up eventually we can get back, plus more.

To survive this enormous economy crunch, maybe our American culture needs to get back to having integrity instead of thinking we need everything in sight that puts us in debt. Moreover, maybe we need to go back and live by that old profound adage, "A man is rich according to what he is, not according to what he has." And maybe we should not have too much pride to keep us from becoming proud.

IS MONEY WORTH STOOPING FOR?

The other day a young man was standing in front of me at the bank and I noticed, when pulling his hand from his pocket, several coins hit the tiled floor with a "clink" and spun around his feet like a top before stopping. He looked down, but never bothered to stoop to pick up his three pennies. I guess they weren't worth it.

Money not being worth stooping for took on a new meaning for me since visiting the Bureau of Engraving and Printing in Washington D.C. a couple of years ago. I received a great education on the Bureau's beginning. Also, the informational tour made me appreciate every red cent! (Pennies are reddish because they are made from copper.)

Junior at the US Mint Headquarters, Washington D.C.

In August of 1862, the actual building of the Bureau of Engraving and Printing was merely a single basement room of the main Treasury building. The work employed six people, two men and four women. Their job was to separate and seal (by hand) one and two dollar bills, or also known as United States Notes. Private bank note companies had previously printed them. Now today, nearly 2,500 are employed and there are two buildings in Washington, D.C., plus a new building established in 1991 in Fort Worth, Texas.

The Bureau tours have all kinds of information for one to read. One fascinating story I remember was about an employee back in 1865. She was a little girl just shy of turning eleven years old. Her name was Emma Brown. She was the youngest worker for the Bureau. Emma's family consisted of herself, along with her disabled mother and older brother, which made him his mother and sister's sole provider, but he decided to enter the military and become a soldier. Unfortunately, he was killed in battle in 1864. That next year, a Congressman heard about the family plight, how now a young daughter was left to care for her physically handicapped mother. To ease the family burden, they hired young Emma Brown. Emma retired 59 years later as a foreman of the trimming department.

Don't you love inspirational stories like that?

I particularly remember the trimming department when touring the Bureau with my husband, son and his family. We were walking on a catwalk, which is elevated so one can look across through the safety glass and see the nearby employees at work. Often workers teased the tourists, acting like they were attempting to steal stacked sheets of money. Of course, you learn with the umpteen production steps and security, embezzling is highly impossible. Besides, it's of no avail because the money is not yet made complete. But most workers liked to amuse visitors walking by. I remember one insistently pointing to a hand written sign hanging on the wall behind his head. I still laugh because it read "I just printed my entire life's salary in less than 1 minute!"

The production process of paper currency is complicated however, and involves over 65 separate and distinct steps. If ever in Washington D.C., take that tour.

Now back to picking up pennies. I understand because of the rising metal prices (like copper), the U.S. Mint now produces some coins at a loss. Therefore they are planning to discontinue making our precious penny. This is because it costs money to make money. In fact, last I read, it costs about 2.5 cents to make a penny and 11 cents to make a nickel. Whoa! …Does that mean our good old nickel is next? The dime is not drowning in debt yet, for it is costing us less than 6 cents. Quarters are still standing perky at less than half price, only costing eleven cents to make. Now, personally, I haven't seen those one-dollar coins for some time, but I hope they stop making them. They are easily mistaken for quarters. Besides, the last I read they cost 25 cents more to produce than our dear old one-dollar paper bill.

What about the price of making our paper money? Apparently, it costs only 5 cents to make a one dollar bill and 8 cents to make both five and ten dollar bills. Also both 20 and 50 dollar bills cost 9 cents. Lastly, the grand finale, the one hundred dollar bill costs a scant 11 pennies.

My goodness, I stepped over about one-fourth of that amount, three pennies, just the other day at the bank! Appreciating money now, I thought of stooping and adopting that guy's poor, meaningless money, but it never seemed appropriate with him standing right there. It would felt like stealing behind his back. But I don't know, maybe our good old American pride has made it so we no longer stoop for pennies.

Decorating & Landscaping

I SHOULD NOT HAVE DONE THAT

Okay, being a home decorator, I don't expect you to agree with or even understand the following story, but I accredit it to when I discovered my exceptional love for home sweet home. I am absolutely passionate about beautifying and creating a home environment. In fact, so much so that I begged my husband the very morning after we got married (on our honeymoon, mind you!), to turn our car around and go home so I could grocery shop and start cooking and decorating with all our wedding gifts. He was perplexed, but being the great guy he is, he was willing. I know that story is abnormal, but I am not exaggerating even a little... that is how eager my love for homemaking is.

Even more shocking is what I did when I first discovered my love for decorating at age thirteen.

My parents had just moved into a small house. I remember how proud I was living there. Never before did we have a sidewalk. But this wasn't just any sidewalk. This was a quaint walkway that made a fun little twist as it led up to our front door. And there in our entry cement slab, embedded with colorful cat-eyed marbles, read the word WELCOME. I remember before entering, I would look behind me at the little white picketed fence around the perimeter of our lush green lawn that made me feel like for the first time I was surrounded by heaven.

And once you walked through our home's front door, the eye-catcher was our living room walls. They were solid knotty pine, lacquered in a high sheen, making them glow. A glow that matched my great feeling! I could go on and on through each room about how proud I was to call this small 2-bedroom house our home.

One evening my parents were gone and I was watching the popular Dick Van Dyke Show with Mary Tyler Moore. How they decorated their home enthralled me. I found myself fascinated by the different ways furniture could be arranged in a living room. For those of you who remember, Mary placed their couch away from the wall and more out in the middle of the living room. And in every episode, Dick was famous for walking in the front door and tripping, doing a somersault over the couch because his walking path had been changed.

Well, taking a good look around our living room, I was motivated to move our couch out from under the window and update the feel of our living room like the movie stars did. So I tugged and pushed and grunted and scooted the couch until I had it nearer to the middle of the room. When that was done, feeling hugely satisfied, I wiped my hands together and thought that was fun! Where else could I redecorate? Where else but my small bedroom! So, full of energy, off I raced.

Looking around my very small sleeping quarters with squinted eyes, studying how everything felt crammed together, it was a no-brainer. I definitely needed more room. Peeking into my parent's bedroom, it was obvious that moving in there would solve my problem.

So walking back into my old bedroom, knowing I did not have the strength to move my set of trundle beds, I decided to let my parents have them. I'd take their big bed. (For those of you who don't know what trundle beds are, they are like a low set of bunk beds on small wheels, one so low it can be rolled under the other when not in use).

That evening, I finished hanging my clothes loosely in my new spacious closet and tightly tucking my parents' clothes in my old one. Did I mention I also didn't have the strength to move bedroom dressers? Well, once I had my clothes neatly folded and nicely spread out in my new spacious, mirrored dresser, I finished cramming my parents' belongings in my old tiny chest of drawers. Lastly, I neatly lined-up my favorite stuffed animals on what felt like an acre of new bed, and I swear they were all smiling at me! Just as I finished, my parents arrived home again.

Walking out to greet them, I was excited to show what was to be my first real decorating experience. But before I could get my enthusiasm off my face, my mother, who was a very practical woman, scowled at me and loudly inquired ..."What in the (bleep) is the couch doing out there in the middle of the living room?" Trying to explain how on the Dick Van Dyke Show they have their couch positioned, she interrupted, "I don't care how Dick Van Dyke puts his couch! You get that couch moved back where it belongs!"

Immediately all my decorating enthusiasm melted. Worse off, fear struck me. What was she going to do when she saw their new sleeping arrangements?

While I was out in the living room grunting and groaning and managing to slowly slide the couch back in place as I was ordered, I sneaked a peek of them opening the wrong bedroom door. Having my shoulders all scrunched up and my lips stretched tight with my eyes squinting and plugging my ears, I held my breath waiting to hear my mother yell some more explicit words. But here is the craziest thing of all. Instead, she and my dad backed out of the bedroom, mumbling something and walked into the only other bedroom. I waited and I waited. I waited for what felt like forever. When I heard the bottom trundle roll out and saw the slim line of light beneath the door to their new bedroom go black, I safely crept into my newly decorated surroundings and slept like a princess. And just like in the storybooks, we all lived happily ever after!

Now I warned you, I never expected you to agree with or even fathom why I got away with that. Because the more I matured, even I was bewildered. It wasn't that I was a spoiled child. However, it may have had something to do with my being their youngest of 16 children ... and the only child left at home. My dad was age 73 and my mother was nudging her 60's when that happened. Truthfully, I believe they were too tuckered out to deal with me.

I warned you that it might be hard to believe, but yes, I did that, which may explain why I later was bold enough to request we cut our honeymoon short.

I convinced my husband no hotel or even castle could create a romantic retreat compared to what I was going to do for us! So, "Why waste our time and money?" was my reasoning.

I shouldn't have done those things; I know that now. And I know I was all about me! But what's a Montana woman to do if she is not doing what she is absolutely passionate about?

Don't answer that ...because this wild wife is not changing!

SPA BATHROOM SAVINGS

Is a bathroom remodel on your list of home improvements? Creating an extravagant spa-like bathroom without an astronomical bill is possible. Here is how you too, can build your dream bathroom on a budget.

Staying in hotels while traveling in Montana, out of state and even other countries, taught my husband and me what we wanted when remodeling our bathroom. Most hotel bathrooms are boring cubicles, a tub-shower unit, toilet and double sinks. In London everything was old and beautifully ornate, but the squeezed–in single sink and toilet were near saucer-sized, hardly big enough for a child. In Cancun and Maui the restful resorts with spacious spa-like bathrooms made one want to linger longer in their lavish atmosphere. That became our remodeling choice.

Spa bathroom

Besides from traveling, other bathroom remodeling ideas came from home shows, internet, decorating magazines and watching HGTV. But taking time to plan is vital. Enjoy the journey of planning your bathroom remodel. Take photos. Clip and save magazine pictures and slip them in a labeled file. Expensive mistakes may be avoided (like installing a pool-size jetted tub) if time is taken to thoroughly research the pros and cons of each element on your wish list. Not being in a rush will allow you to define your priorities, financially and style-wise, and figure out where to cut costs and where to splurge. After my friend's three-story home was built she missed her quick relaxing bath. She found filling their huge jetted tub takes time and volumes of water. They are now replacing their expensive tub for a simple tub that fits their needs.

Our most wanted spa item was a stone walk-in shower. Creating additional space for the least expense caused us to explore our options. Rather than expanding from the exterior wall, we took space from our large dining room next door. We opted not to spend big bucks on several showerheads shooting from all directions. Instead, the single rainfall showerhead pan and hand-held shower bar were sufficient. However, buying high-end and quality fixtures and faucets needs to be everyone's priority, whether that's euro-shaped spouts arched high over glass bowls or standard spouts over farmhouse or regular sinks. One popular plumbing company advertises, "Buy it for looks. Buy it for life." That's true. Cheaper fixtures peel, break and need replaced often, costing more in the long run.

Spa bathroom

We removed our 1970s tub and shower unit and created an area with its own romantic ambiance. When decorating, my husband always selects our wall art and then I create the décor or atmosphere around it. Surprisingly, he chose this large picture of a stylish couple dancing on the ocean shore - a romantic reminder of years before when we danced on an evening dinner cruise in New York, and then later in London. Calling for a dance floor atmosphere, I envisioned a cove under double archways with elegant lighting directly above the bathtub. You'll notice the pillars in the photo. You may be surprised to know they were created with PVC pipe! Improvising in this way can potentially save a substantial amount of money or allow you to splurge elsewhere in your remodel.

Spas are meant to spoil us. Stepping on a walk-in shower floor composed of small glazed rocks becomes an instant foot massage and feels glorious to tired feet. If that's not a priority, there are many spa inspired flooring options and bath mats available at very affordable prices. Perhaps a thick grass mat sold at Bed Bath & Beyond will tantalize your feet. They also make foam rugs that feel like forest moss.

Speaking of feet, heated floor tiles are wonderful for freezing Montana winters. But should something electrical go wrong, floor tiles may need to be torn up. We opted not to take that financial risk. However, still wanting warm tiles, we improvised by heightening the base under our double-sink unit and the electrician placed two heaters with a wall thermostat. Our earthy colored tiled floor is warm in an instant…and the savings difference is a sin to talk about!

For us, double sinks were a must. And above the stone counter top we wanted a huge 8 feet by 4 feet mirror encompassing two walls. Mirrors bring magic to a room. Their reflection gives two of everything for the price of one, plus doubling the appearance of the room's size. Mirror is relatively inexpensive. Of course, the more you customize with special cuts or beveling, the higher the cost. In my 'Decorating on a Dime' business, I tell home owners all the time, "You will look the same in an inexpensive mirror as you do in an expensive mirror." Overall room atmosphere is what's noticed - often it's not expensive details. The money you save on mirrors can be allocated to your "priority" list.

When it comes to priorities - plenty of flattering light while standing at the mirror is something every Montana woman wants. Recessed lighting along with hanging light fixtures are what we chose. Choose your light fixtures carefully as they will lend significant impact to the room's style and functionality.

A wall of glass blocks before stepping in the shower may be one area where you want to splurge. And having a window for fresh air. Between the window, glass blocks and big mirrors, the reflection of light makes bathrooms airy and well lit.

Final touches added to a spa bathroom atmosphere are:

Luxurious white towels rolled and neatly placed in a basket or open shelf gives a clean and spa-like look. Towel bars can be expensive and unnecessary. Hooks are handy. They always make towels hang right … and no fuss. But maybe a heated towel rack is your must have!

Popular reed diffusers are in keeping with the look of a spa while keeping the bathroom smelling fresh and clean.

Candles are always a therapeutic, romantic and stylish addition to the bathroom. Set them in a tray with glazed rocks or sand to complement the spa style during the day and enjoy the shadows flickering on the wall in the evening.

Soothing background music is bound to make any spa bathroom a peaceful getaway you won't want to leave.

Again, enjoy the journey. Take time researching all options when remodeling your bathroom into a retreat. It need not be expensive to be exquisite.

LOW PRICED PATIO AND LANDSCAPING

Building a patio and hiring landscaping can cost big bucks. By the time a landscaper comes to our home, designs and does everything, we're talking a good chunk of money. And with today's economy, job cutbacks and less money to live on, who can afford the luxury of a new patio and landscaping?

Well, giving tips on how to save money is my area of expertise! I know how to step inside your home and teach how to decorate on a dime, dress on a dime and dine on a dime, but for the next few minutes let's step outside your home and learn how to deck on a dime or build a patio at a low price, plus do some dirt-cheap landscaping.

Look at the photo of what my husband and I did. That's our low-cost landscaping and penny-pinching patio. Here's how we built a low price

Low priced patio

patio.

Our sidewalk cracked and for safety reasons needed to be replaced. For that job we did hire someone. When he came, I asked if instead of crumbling or jack hammering the concrete, if we paid him would he cut the good concrete into huge slabs setting them aside.

He scratched his head and wondered why. I explained we wanted to build a big patio adjoining the sidewalk and had only so many bricks. By using the previous concrete slabs and adding our few bricks, we would have a spacious patio. And it would very nicely match our new sidewalk. He agreed, although he had never heard of such a thing.

Look at the photo. Obviously, my idea worked. My husband spent time and sweat digging and laying the brick and slab. But the point is that we spent no money on bricks or concrete by reusing our old sidewalk and leftover bricks. A person could do the same with flat rocks or a pile of pavers he may have stacked somewhere. But that's how you build a penny-pinching patio.

Speaking of rocks, now look in the photo's background. See those ever-so-popular rock pillars? Five of them border our yard. We selected rocks from our acreage and fenced them in heavy wire around all five of our old post lights. (Friends are usually happy to let you pick and haul off rocks from their fields.) We incorporated rock because we could not afford new post lights. Be inventive!

We even made a curved rock wall and two for our driveway entrances 3 feet high by 2 feet wide by 11 feet long out of caged rocks. And instead of paying to run electricity out to our driveway entrance, we braced four inexpensive solar lights in the rocks.

Here's a tip. Before placing rocks around posts, or along driveway entrances, hose them clean. After they dry, place them in the wire cage and then spray with a clear acrylic. The gloss enhances the rock colors with a rich luster. They really rock!

Save a bundle by building your own outdoor rock fire pit. At end-of-summer sales, search for an outdoor screened fireplace like we did. They are quite cozy and popular.

The end of July is the best time to start looking for half-priced patio furniture. You may have to mix and match, but it saves money. For instance, we found black iron chairs and spray painted a golden bronze table black to match them.

But hey, if you can't find or afford a table, build your patio around a tall tree stump. Then for a tabletop, cut a circular piece out of thick plywood. Screw it on the stump and evenly lay and adhere a slab-rock top. Possibly incorporate a place for a removable umbrella. Add to the outdoor atmosphere by purchasing (on sale, of course) a tall heat post to keep your company toasty on cool Montana evenings around your outdoor dining.

Also, save money shopping at the end of July for other landscaping items. Fantastic deals are out there on fountains… unless you know how to build your own water feature.

The point is: don't go into debt doing your landscaping. Outdoor living is peaceful, but not if you defeat your purpose and can't afford making payments. Learn patience. Stretch your dollars and stretch out what you want to buy over years.

There is no need to even purchase pricey landscaping books or magazines on how to lay a patio, build a fire pit, or create a water feature. Go online or to your local library and check out material they have. That's what we did.

Get creative. Use and redo what you already have. Revamp what's retired! You'll be surprised. Go snoop in old outbuildings and cart out what you can recreate. Remember, distressed looks, chipped enamels, and rusty textures are in. Use old wicker, but soften it by adding a couple nice pillows. Arrange a trio of old milk cans in a flowerbed. Place old, paint-peeled shutters on the sides of your tool shed window. Underneath the widow, anchor a distressed flower box. Now soften the features by planting variegated vines or pastel flowers that flow down. Have an old wheelbarrow? Use it as a planter.

If your Montana property is timbered land that grows wild shrubs, dig and transplant them. Feed them and watch them grow. Again, that's what we did.

Haul a huge rooted stump to your property. Tip it on its side. With roots upright, pack loads of dirt inside roots crevices. Now plant flowers, add animal antlers and trailing greenery. Or haul a few boulders, place dirt, then add a few plants. Adding a landscape lamp or even solar light would be awesome! See how one idea will give birth to another creative idea?

Montana women, you can create a breathtaking outdoor atmosphere without creating an astronomical bill! Get started and create a yard with a panoramic view. You're bound to get a great review.

In fact, you have just done two things: you increased your home value and you created an outdoor living space at hardly any cost.

Food

&

Exercise

MOVE OVER MARTHA STEWART!

Autumn in Montana is breathtaking with all the colorful foliage. It is my favorite time of the year to invite guests for dinner. Fresh fruit and vegetables are in abundance and make a dinner table inviting at little expense. So move over Martha Stewart! Margie Montana wants her turn.

Today's economy calls for us to fix a fine dinner without spending a fortune, yet without looking frugal. There is no need to have elaborate dinnerware and serve several courses to impress visitors at our table. Learning how to serve food within food will spruce up everyday meals and create a lasting impression that will not break the budget, by using already tried and true recipes ...our heirloom dinners, savory soups, cost-efficient casseroles and budget desserts.

That being said, let's learn how to make more than a meal. Let's make a statement!

Every fall, well-meaning friends weigh us down with an armload of zucchini squash. In fact, my friend Helen Bundrock made me laugh when she said, "I never go to church and leave my car unlocked in the fall. Otherwise I come out and

My late sister Macia Madison in Libby - a great gardener and also a scumptious cook.

140

it's filled with huge zucchini!"

Seriously, what is a person to do with all those free, foot-long, fat monsters? Most of them are as big as serving bowls. Serving bowls... exactly! Cut the zucchini lengthwise, slice a sliver off the bottom to level it and hollow out the inside with an ice cream scoop (for smaller ones, use a melon scoop). Depending on the size, use the zucchini as a serving dish by filling it with cold chicken salad, macaroni, potato or bean salad. A zucchini can also be used as a veggie tray by arranging celery, carrots, broccoli, cauliflower, cucumbers and cherry tomatoes. Smaller zucchini or even cucumbers make perfect boats for olives, shrimp, tarter sauce, sour cream or dips for chips.

Food being served in food is not a new concept. We have all seen watermelon made into a basket complete with handles or a half cantaloupe with a wedged top filled with fruit, tuna salad stuffed in tomatoes, taco salad served in crisp bowl-like shells, and soup served in bread bowls. Following are other ideas using food as a serving dish:

• Many mouth-watering recipes are already in your file, but can be enhanced by being presented in new packaging. For example, to break up the humdrum monotony of the usual platter of hamburgers and hotdogs, serve the following condiments on the side: ketchup in a red pepper skin, mustard in a yellow pepper skin, and relish in a green pepper skin. Thinly slice off the bottoms so each bell pepper is level, place a spoon inside and use the stemmed tops for lids. Place the peppers lined in a row—they show-off better. How easy is that? Guests will rave at your imagination in using food to serve food. And to economize, later rinse, chop, freeze and reuse peppers for your next kettle of chili, pasta sauce or soup.

• Speaking of soup, there is no need to purchase a big, expensive soup tureen. Instead, use an oversized pumpkin. Again, keep the stemmed top for a handy lid. Hollow out the center, and depending on the size, set a serving bowl or kettle inside along with a soup ladle. Toss a few colorful oak or dried maple leaves around the pumpkin's base and you have your centerpiece. For place cards, write the name of each guest on a leaf with a marker and place it in his/her soup bowl. Or for a Halloween soup dinner, hot-glue acorn candies along with assorted hard candies to make a face on the pumpkin, or assemble candy flowers.

• We can also beautify our drinks. Your brunch will earn rave reviews when you take huge cucumbers, square off the bottoms, core out the centers and use them to serve V-8 juice. Your guests will love sipping from these unique green tumblers.

• Try this. Take a large cucumber and core out the center. Push a very slim carrot through the center core and then slice the "stuffed" cucumber with a serrated knife. When guests munch these crisp disks, they will wonder how you accomplished it.

• Once creative juices start flowing, there's no stopping. Use a uniformly shaped eggplant or butternut squash as a floral vase and fill lavishly with asters or sunflowers. Guests, seeing our picture perfect autumn centerpiece, will no doubt think "you are the hostess with the mostest"! And you will know it certainly didn't take that much money. There is also no need to explain that you will be eating that vase in a delicious soup later.

• Speaking of centerpieces – cored and leveled large, somewhat green tomatoes or apples make candleholders for long stem candles at evening meals. Stuff leafy parsley around the hole after candle is inserted to hold it tightly.

• Take a huge unpeeled apple, core out a wide center, and then rinse in lemon juice (this prevents the inside of the apple from browning). Now you have the ideal dish for jelly or apple butter for your pork roast dinner. For dessert, fill a cored apple with caramel sauce to drizzle over ice cream.

• Kids love Jiggle Jell-O, those rubbery, sweet squares that don't melt in little hands. Instead of using an oblong cake pan, pour liquid lime Jell-O into halved, thick orange or grapefruit rinds. Chill until firm. Then, using a serrated knife cut fruit halves into wedges and arrange on a bed of lettuce. Even big fingers will grab these tasty Jell-O slices still in the rind.

• All ages love chocolate bowls. Over a deep narrow double boiler, barely melt chocolate candy pieces. Have ready some medium-sized round inflated balloons. Take a tablespoon of melted chocolate and pour onto waxed paper. (The chocolate circle will serve as the balloon's base.) Now, dip the inflated balloon about halfway down into the warm chocolate, tipping it to the north, south, east and west. Pull the balloon straight up out of the chocolate and allow it to drip. You will have a nice scalloped edge. Set balloon on the chocolate base to cool into a hardened shell. Taking a straight pin, carefully poke the balloon at the "navel" where it is tied, then help the air seep slowly out. Gently remove the deflated balloon. And voila! Desserts in chocolate bowls are to die for. Serve banana splits, strawberry shortcake or brownies and ice cream. You name it!

To make your meal even more memorable, show some front porch hospitality. Serve dinner on the porch this fall. Or take your dining table and chairs down by the creek, the shady side of the red barn, or under the big oak tree. Montana's October outdoors becomes your formal dining room with cloth napkins, silverware, and stemmed glassware (from the Dollar Store). We often see this setting in magazines and wish we were there.

Finally, we need to bow our heads and thank our Lord that we live in Montana, America, the beautiful land of spacious skies and plenty. And be thankful for family and friends … even those who load us down with an armload of zucchini. Remember Helen Bundrock's statement about keeping her car locked in the fall because friends will fill it with zucchini? When sharing her humor with my late sister Marcia Madison (in the photo), who was a great gardener and marvelous cook, she quipped back, "Well, they say, 'you know you don't have any friends when you go to the grocery store and have to buy zucchini.'"

EXERCISE? I PREFER CHOCOLATE

Seriously, exclude me! Every time I even say the word "exercise" I immediately want to rinse my mouth out with chocolate. I detest the word, let alone the thought of going to the gym.

Are there any Montana women out there who relate with me? Or am I the only anti-gym gal in the state? Well, I'm coming out of the closet to stake my claim. Okay, I've been this way all my life. When in school, I was one of those girls in P.E. class who stood around with arms folded across her waist, totally uninvolved. My body language of protecting myself never made A's on my report card, let alone protected me. For instance: One day in gym class playing kick ball, a classmate named Pat came plowing towards me like a workhorse. She had her eyes fixed on the ball that happened to be resting at my feet beneath my crossed arms. It never occurred to me to kick the ball. Before I knew it, Pat's muscular leg came at me. She missed the ball whacking me right above the ankle. I crashed to the floor with excruciating pain and immediate swelling surrounding my injury. I limped for weeks. In fact, a year later I still wore a badly bruised, egg-shaped hard lump on my shin. That experience confirmed I had no business being in any kind of gym class.

Why some gals find it fun to go to a fitness center is beyond me. I have absolutely no patience for the wasted time, money and physical exertion spent. Perhaps others out there feel the same but fear the shame of being a rare woman in our saturated culture of fitness.

So if you are a lover of working out at a fitness center or if you have specific doctor orders to exercise, read no further. This article will explain alternate forms of exercise for women who detest that "E" word as much as I do. It's also for those who can't afford the money or spent time in a fitness center, but want to learn ways to stay physically fit without a gym membership.

I share the following with confidence of being in my 70s and the same size as the day I was badly kicked in high school gym class. All right, at my age I admit to some sagging skin. Going from bra size 36C to 36 Long comes with gravity. Can't help it!

Here is how to keep fit without a fitness center and get needed jobs at home done while you exercise. Why ride a stationary bike that takes you nowhere? Get on one that goes somewhere! You know, like to buy groceries. Why lift weights when you can carry grocery bags and strengthen your biceps instead of those belonging to the store employee carrying your groceries.

Instead of using a rowing machine, sit on the floor with a pile of unfolded laundry. Place the pile in front of your toes so some serious reaching is required. Another option is to sit with your legs crossed, reach and stretch, working your inner thighs. Spending energy on accomplishing household jobs makes more sense to me. I have found (in my decorating bedrooms) that oftentimes the home exercise equipment soon becomes a clothes rack.

For better balance, rethink standing and folding laundry. Unless it is a tall front-loader type, use the dryer top as a table. Now squat, doing a deep knee bend each time you reach inside the dryer drum for a single item to fold. Or balance on one leg and kick the other leg straight back when going down. Again, love the fact you are finishing the laundry while getting in better physical shape.

If your home has a staircase, rethink how you already have a built-in stair master. Create ways to get house or office work done by using stairs often throughout the day. Never just set items on the steps to be taken upstairs on your next trip. Instead, immediately take each item up individually. Well-spent time at home will benefit you.

Moving continually morning till night is the key to staying in shape. Speaking of morning till night, even how you cleanse and moisturize your face and neck can help a double chin. Simply tilt your head way back. Look straight at the ceiling. Now apply face cream and stroke upward. Then while neck is stretched upward, open mouth wide and close it slowly. You will definitely feel it!

Oh and here's another one that is good for the heart. It is my wild wife secret! Did you know that every time you kiss you actually burn 9 calories? Goodness, that's a great way to burn energy. My husband always winks and sways his way across the floor requesting a kiss that will burn 30 calories! The guy in your life will love this exercise.

Yikes! Did I say the word "exercise?" I'm out of here. I need to go rinse my mouth out with chocolate. I might as well lean my head way back and gargle that chocolate too. Bending back for chocolate has got to be beneficial! That's my rethinking now that I am out of the closet.

Holidays
Family Fun
and Humor

'SPRINGTIME IN THE ROCKIES'

The late John Denver may have sung "Springtime in the Rockies," but I threw the party! And you can too. Gals, here is a creative idea for a reunion planned from your Montana Home Sweet Home. If you have a large family, host a chick party. It is a clever way to keep female cousins or maybe even all your Montana High School girlfriends connected. Whether you have a big or small group of gals, you can pull this off. Last spring was my 5th one. Each reunion or party has an entirely different theme. One was a Pampered Party. Forty of us gals went to Montana Athletic Club here in Libby to exercise, have massages and enjoy make-up classes. That afternoon, my brother whose name is Montana and who was once a chef, cooked a delicious meal for us.

Backing-up a bit… being the youngest of 16 siblings, I like keeping my huge family with all our female cousins and aunts connected to their Montana roots. Cousins are wide spread throughout the U.S. and may only meet because of a family funeral. And because life guarantees us all sad times, I wanted us to create some happy times as well.

Here's an abbreviated version of the invitation I sent. Just tweak the ideas to fit your own needs for a family or girlfriend gathering.

~~~~~~~~~~~~~~~

It's Time for the Hutton Cousin Chick Party!

April 23rd-26th needs to be highlighted in chick yellow on your calendar. We only do this every 5 years, so don't miss out. And now is the time for getting great airfares.

Can you believe this will be our 5th one? Each party has a different theme and this one is "Springtime in the Rockies." I would love to spill all the jelly beans about what we will be doing, but you will be handed a complete agenda once here. But first things first!

This is the hardest part for me to mention, so let's make it first. Because there are many young nieces coming up, please make sure they are age 15 before they attend. This is not planned for younger ages. Certainly if you are a nursing mom, tuck baby under wing and don't miss coming.

Remember: Ages 15-19 are Chickadees, ages 20-49 are Chicks, ages 50-79 are Hens. At age 80 you get to start all over by becoming a Pullet because we may have to help PULL you out of the car and help PULL you off the couch! No Stewing Hens allowed.

Chick Party Theme: Springtime in the Rockies

What are you to pack in your suitcase to protect your Fluffy Feathers?

Because it is springtime and we will be outdoors much of the time, rain gear is probably needed. Pack nothing too dressy. Go online and see our weather forecast. You don't want to get soaked and look like an ugly duckling.

Girl Cousin Chick Party!

Also don't forget to pack an item or two for our fun Cousin Clothing Exchange. Bring something(s) you no longer wear. Our past clothes rummaging pile was a big hit. Remember, we all come in different sizes...from fluffy to few feathers. And some have tall drumsticks and some have short drumsticks. Some are big breasted and some aren't bragging! But plan to toss some item in our pile to be pecked through.

Also remember we have a gift exchange. Buy one and keep it at around $15.

One more thing to pack: family photos. It is extremely important you bring them. Time is set up for us to reproduce prints. Everyone can go home with relatives' photos, from great-great-great grandparents to aunts, uncles and cousins. Don't miss-out giving and receiving photos of our heritage.

When do we first meet?
Fly or waddle in Thursday, April 23rd and fly or waddle out Sunday, April 26th.

Where do we Roost?
Libby Venture Inn and Restaurant. Everyone will pay or split room cost with other chick(s). So, please make your own nesting arrangements.

What happens once we arrive in Libby on Thursday?

6 PM Kick-off:
Meet at the SOUP COUP for dinner. That is my home, Aunt Margie. (Address and phone number) As usual I will stuff you with Grandma Hutton's Homemade Chick N' Noodle Soup. (Sorry she never made it with beef). We will also have our traditional Bean Soup so we can tip a cup to all those 'party poopers' who never came! Warm cheesy bread and yummy desserts will also be served.

Thursday night you will be handed a printed agenda with details on times and everything we will be doing on Friday and Saturday.

When is it all over?

Plan to drive, fly, waddle or drag home on Sunday.

So come join us whether you are silly or shy. You will find a comfortable place being the chick you are; either perched and quietly chuckling or strutting and noisily clucking.

~~~~~~~~~~~~~~~

Once they arrived, a detailed agenda for the weekend was given to everyone. Our weekend was filled with a Hoola Hoop Coup contest, a Barn Yard fashion show, a bus tour into the nearby Yaak country to have lunch on the river and a photo taken with Sasquatch. Saturday night we have live music (Sing to the tune "Turkey in the Straw") and line dance to:

'I'm a bow-legg'd chicken, I'm a knock-knee'd hen
Never been so happy since I don't know when
I walk with a wiggle and giggle and a squawk
Doin' the Montana Wigwalk.

To the tune of a fiddle on a hardwood floor
Tho' I'm broke and I'm weary and my back is sore
I walk with a wiggle and giggle and a squawk
Doin' the Montana wigwalk.

Put your toes together; your knees apart
Bend your back, get ready to start
Flap your elbows just for luck
Then you wiggle and you waddle
Like a baby duck.
Doin' the Montana Wigwalk!

Come Sunday morning we will all go our separate ways, but they won't forget their Montana roots!

HALLOWEEN WITH OR AWAY
FROM GRANDKIDS

I've heard said, "Having grandkids is like a can of pop. We shake them up and then hand them back to their parents!" Of course, that's when we slip off to bed and sleep like a baby.

Yep, we have the fun of not having all the work of raising them, but all the wild fun of running ragged with them. What a reward! All of us grandparents know what fun these little curtain climbers can be.

Do you have plans with your young grandkids this Halloween? You know, sugar them up and then hand them back to their parent to explode?

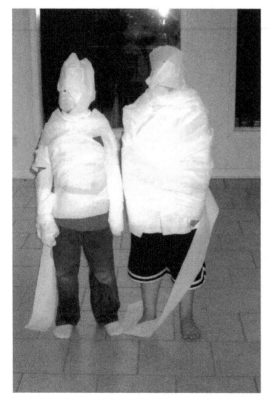

Grandkids, 2008

Because I am a long distant grandma, I don't get to be with mine very often. Therefore I celebrate every occasion every chance I get, whether that be earlier in the year or by mail and even in hotel rooms. Becoming creative has become my calling. Otherwise I'd miss out. I find even the simplest things like mailing a package of Candy Corns calms my long distant longings and creates a memory.

But making memories are what we grandmas love and do best. That's true whether we live miles away from them in Montana or just across the street.

Here are some Halloween ideas that fit all situations, whether we are a long distance grandma, traveling with them in a hotel, or having them in your home... or even if you choose to celebrate early in their home. (We've celebrated Easter early and Christmas late.)

If you are a long distance grandma, mail them a gift certificate to Pizza Hut or McDonalds, or a favorite bookstore, or money to buy their Halloween costume.

Maybe you are going to be with them around Halloween, but you are traveling with them and in a hotel. Here's how we've celebrated:

Using toilet tissue, we wrapped our grandchildren Cody and Conner into mummies. That was a favorite fun thing to do when they were younger. In fact, they bugged us to twirl them around in toilet tissue even as they grew and were older and it's not even Halloween!

But if traveling, before going to the hotel, go to the grocery store and buy pumpkin muffins and a can of frosting, along with candy to decorate their own treat in the hotel room.

Also Dollar Stores often have wash cloths that come packaged the size of a silver dollar and are stamped with different designs. Once at the hotel, let them each set their own in a basin of warm water and watch it immediately grow to actual size.

How about getting in on the fun? Purchase face paint and hair gel and let them make you the creature! See how handy that stamped washcloth will become? That way you won't leave the hotel management the mess.

Perhaps you could sneak buying a not-so-scary mask and jump out from behind the shower curtain while they are at the sink using their washcloths. Grandkids love grandparents doing weird and unexpected things.

For a hotel game, cut out a large pumpkin from orange construction paper and several small pumpkin stems from green construction paper. Now blindfold each player. Twirl them around. Using Scotch tape on the pumpkin stem, have every player stick the stem on the pumpkin. (It's like the game Pin the Tail on the Donkey.) Whoever gets closest to the middle on the pumpkin top wins.

Then of course, for a bedtime story they love hearing about Halloweens that you or their mommy or daddy celebrated when they were young like them.

When hugging them good night, end the evening with a Halloween joke. Tell your grandchild to say, "Terrified." And now have them say, "Tissue." Now tell them to say both words together quickly. After they blurt out, "Terrified tissue!" (Care if I kiss you?), you reach over and give your big Grandma smooch.

You may be blessed to have them in your home or you're at their home this Halloween. Internet or October household magazines provide a host of projects. With little older kids, you can teach them anything from baking and decorating creepy bugs to carving fingers out of hot dogs. Think eating finger hot dogs is too gross? Your little goblins will have no trouble gobbling a chocolate frosted jellyroll cake made into a rotting log with vanilla pudding oozing out along with gummy worms!

Make an entire day of Halloween if you can. With very young children who are just learning their colors, tell them for dinner everything has to be orange. Then let them help. Maybe suggest spaghetti topped with cheese, orange Jello, carrots and orange frosted sugar cookies.

Do you want to have real fun?! Once dinner is cooked and ready to eat, announce, "We are going to do a Backward Night." Crawl out of bed, say your prayers, walk backwards to the bathroom, brush your teeth, walk backwards to the dinner table, eat dessert first, and then eat dinner last!

And if they don't get their veggies down because they are too full ... then that's fine! And now that they are fused like fireworks or fizzing like a can of shaken pop... that's their parents' problem to handle. Besides, by now you are too tuckered out! You need to go off to bed. Their parents can calm all the bottled-up fizz and fussing. You've had your fun!

What better way to treat your grandkids and trick your grown kids?

DADDY WANTS SOME LOVIN'

Our family tradition when our boys were young, was fixing Thanksgiving dinner on our antique cast iron wood cookstove. That was the only day my husband cooked in the kitchen with me. I did all the side dishes, desserts, table setting and cleaning up. His job was merely making his delicious dressing and stuffing the bird to the gills. As soon as Mr. Tom was shoved in our old wood cookstove, my husband was ready to play! (Actually he was a nuisance.) Often he'd hand our boys pots, lids and spoons to bang with while marching them around the house singing his made-up version of some silly song.

One Thanksgiving morning after the turkey was in the oven and my

husband was wild to play, he wanted me out of the kitchen, wanting my total attention. (Some of you Montana women know exactly what I am talking about.) This could amount to smooching, dancing ... to even a tickling contest in the middle of the living room floor with the entire family ending up in a dog pile.

Strutting toward me across the kitchen floor and winking, he pulled out his wood turkey caller, an actual gobble box, smiling, "Honey, watch the boys come running in here. Go along with me. This will be fun!"

My wood cookstove

So I did. Nerve racking as it was, I never complained when he started rattling by jiggling the screeching wooden chalk box that cackles, sounding like some male turkey making a love-call, requesting his mate. And of course just as he predicted, our boys immediately came rushing into the kitchen to investigate the noise. Still winking, my husband swooned me in further by being in his "making-up-a-new-song-mood," singing "Gobble, gobble, gobble…Happy Thanksgiving Day. Turkey's in the oven and Daddy wants some lovin'…Happy Thanksgiving Day."

"Okay boys," he requested, "if Daddy is going to get any kissin' out of Mommy, then help me sing this song. Travis you go first."

And of course, Travis eagerly sang just like his Daddy worded it. But when our youngest son Kevin sang, his words were just as enthusiastic but incorrect as he bellowed…. "Gobble, gobble, gobble…Happy Thanksgiving Day. Daddy's in the oven and the turkey wants some lovin'…Happy Thanksgiving Day."

Busting out in laughter, we thought his version was hilarious, while Kevin never understood his innocent mistake. Travis just patted his little brother on the back and assured him he put the right turkey in the oven!

Even though that happened many, many Thanksgivings ago, that song became our family tradition. In fact, now our young grandsons phone us early every Thanksgiving morning long distance to sing the wrong version.

Be grateful for family traditions at Thanksgiving. They encourage feelings of closeness and strengthen our family bond. So if you have not made some, start this year. And whether they are serious or fun, they are important. Traditions are what hold us together. They remind us of our family background. Our upbringing. Our way of life. What we experienced. The things we practiced.

Gotta go. Mr. Hot Wings is calling his wild wife …he's still wanting some huggin'!

TRUSTING YOUR THANKSGIVING HOSTESS

I love family and friends who have a great sense of humor. Some are so hilarious they double me over in a good belly laugh. In fact, I asked my best friend who snapped this photo if I could share it for a Thanksgiving story. I even offered to keep her name out to protect her innocence, but she didn't care. She knows how to laugh at herself. Don't you just love family and friends like that? We all have them!

Take a close look at that turkey ready to be carved. Did you notice the kitchen sink plug? Now if you are like me, my biggest bowl for scrubbing and filling my twenty-pound turkey is my scoured kitchen sink. Seriously, my girlfriend Donna Bundrock Greenup, who is a great cook, did just that. After stuffing the turkey, she plopped the bird in to be baked, not knowing the kitchen sink plug was stuck.

If you were Donna, now do you or don't you tell your dinner guests?

Knowing Donna like I do, if dinner guests were to ask for her delicious dressing recipe, with her sense of humor, she'd probably be honest and say, "Oh, I just added everything but the kitchen sink!"

My girlfriend Donna roasted a turkey and when they went to carve it they found the kitchen sink drain plug.

Showing that turkey photo to a gal the other day, I wanted to see if the photo would strike her with humor, like it did me. Instead, her seriousness gave me a second laugh as she took the photo in hand and eagerly inquired, "Oh is using a sink plug now a new way of holding in turkey stuffing?" Honestly, she was ready to try it!

EASTER BUNNY EVIDENCES

The door slammed, jarring my grandsons' bed. "Wake up! Wake up!" I screamed. "Grandma J believes the Easter Bunny was here!"

Cody and Conner immediately sprang up, twisting their little fists in their blinking eyes, trying to envision what was happening.

Now that I had them on their feet, I unfolded what we needed to do. Placing my finger over my lips, very quietly I shared, "Today is Easter and I believe the Easter Bunny was here. There will be three evidences if he was. Let's find out." (Evidences is a big word for eager little ears to learn.)

Stumbling right upon my heels, they knelt beside me at the door where white footprints left the room. That's when I started lecturing, "Understand, the Easter Bunny is made of all sugar and if this white stuff is sweet, it's probably his powered sugared footprints."

Sure enough, my oldest grandson Cody dipped his finger and sampled it on his tongue, squealing, "Yeah, Grandma J, it's sweet!"

"Well, we just found evidence #1!" I rejoiced. Slowly standing up, I further instructed, "Boys, don't touch the door. First, search the door very closely. Do you see any other evidences?"

Again, Cody's keen little eyes spotted the chunk of cotton (candy) clinging to the door's casing. Caught up in his searching, he shouted, "Look! What's this?"

"Evidence #2! I cheered. "That's gotta be part of his cottontail. It must have got caught in the door when he slammed it." They quickly agreed, hopping around like rabbits themselves!

"Okay, calm down. This is important," bringing them back around.

Cody and Conner, July 2002

"What will we find on the other side of this door?"

Slowly, with great anticipation, I turned the doorknob, edging the door open. And there on the floor was a mound of colorful jelly beans.

Conner, my youngest, immediately fell on his knees and had a handful of candy stuffed in his mouth before I could explain, "That's evidence #3! We know the Easter Bunny is made of sugar and he must have got so-o scared, he 'pottied' jelly beans before he fled." Again, to these little believers, that made perfect sense.

Seeing my grandchildren filling their little chubby cheeks with candy and drooling colors of the rainbow before breakfast did my grandmother's heart good.

Lastly, I coached them to follow the trail of white footprints and they'd find their Easter baskets at the end.

Have fun this Easter with your little 'energized bunnies'. Make magical Montana moments with them. And remember... We don't spend time with our grandkids, we invest it.

[Thanks to my good friend Kathleen Sheffield, who shared this idea years ago. Now I pass it on.]

WILD WIFE—THE VENGEFUL VALENTINE

A few years back, the newspaper read, "Love to be Wacky Contest. Win an out-of-town weekend for two including lodging, dinner and entertainment." All I had to do was write in "The wackiest thing I ever did to prove to my spouse that I loved him."

Well, my wackiest was really on the verge of being my revenge! However, my payback did turn into a loving wrestling match in the middle of our living room floor, so why not try to win this romantic weekend? After all, my husband did deserve winning something for my mischievousness. So I mailed my wacky, wild, romantic story and won!

Here's that winning Valentine story:

One evening, my husband Junior promised to watch a romantic movie with me. I got all cuddled in my corner of the couch and Junior got all stretched out. In fact, his feet were on my lap.

I thought I'd quickly paint my fingernails. But before my nails were painted and even before the movie's theme music was over, Junior had already fallen asleep. Sitting there in disgust, and with his feet practically propped in my face and snoring like a 747 jet roaring to take off, I was instantly mad!

Painting finger nails

Instead of reacting and interfering with his sleep, I decided to do the Biblical thing. I did "unto him what I would want done unto me." I painted all his toenails cherry red!

Well, I knew I had painted ten cherry bombs ready to explode once he set eyes on his toes. However, his toes went unnoticed that night. Blurry eyed, he found his way to bed and slept beautifully.

Early the next morning, I eagerly sneaked in and woke up our two young sons. I wanted to include them in all my upcoming fun.

So waiting patiently in the hallway, we kept peeping around the corner, waiting for the sleeping giant to wake up. And just like I predicted, he swung his feet over the side of the bed, and when he viewed his grotesque feet... boy, oh boy... the fireworks started! The battle was on.

The wild chase through the house ended with Junior tackling me in the living room, tickling me nearly to tears. So, my romantic revenge ended just like I wanted...with Junior winning the battle with a beautiful de-feet!

As a Montana wild wife, with many years of marriage, I still don't like for my husband to ever think he has me fully figured out. I believe we have a power in the mystery of being a woman. Besides, I think my husband married me to be a little entertained. And to this very day, he does have a healthy fear of me when it comes to watching romantic movies.

Montana woman, I hope you find some romantic, wild, wacky way to keep your husband on his toes. Keep that spark of fascination and fun in your marriage and family, because families who laugh together, last together.

CUTTING THE APRON STRINGS

Hey, Montana Mom, do you have a wedding coming up? Let me share something I did when our son got married.

The rehearsal dinner was about to begin. As mother-of-the-groom, I had planned little extra things to make the dinner more special. And because the wedding was out of state, I added a little Montana for our son Travis. Certainly the DVD of him growing up in the great outdoors of Northwest Montana would help accomplish that!

My soon-to-be daughter-in-law,Charele had chosen a deep royal purple as her accent color, so adding a tray of beautiful purple tin-foiled, yummy huckleberry cordials at the guest book would work perfectly.

I even dressed in a purple outfit, wearing a crème laced apron. (You can buy one. They are specifically made for mother-of-the-groom rehearsal dinners.)

And speaking of aprons... let me take you on a quick side trip. I am not an "apron woman". However, once my son was engaged to Charele, I started wearing this meaningless blue apron that hung unused in my pantry. I made certain I wore it every time Charele was in our home. I wanted her to connect it with me as

Travis and Charele

part of my kitchen attire.

Now back to this rehearsal dinner. Everything on my part as mother-of-the-groom was going as planned. Guests entered the room and while signing in and waiting in their designated seats they enjoyed eating the attractively purple-wrapped Montana huckleberry chocolates. Then the DVD of our son growing up fishing and hiking in the Cabinet Mountain Wilderness made a memorable statement to all those living in the flatland of Kansas where their wedding was taking place.

Now for my soon-to-be-daughter-in-law...I had something important and memorable planned for her also. After my husband played the DVD for our son, he read a funny poem he wrote for her. He expressed humor about how important he would be in his new role as father-in-law and how nicely she would treat him, calling him over early every morning for a delicious homemade breakfast!

After the video and the funny poem the laughter subsided. I then walked over and standing behind Charele's chair, I leaned down and kissed her on the cheek. I then set a small two-inch, beautifully wrapped purple box with a neatly tied ivory bow on her dinner plate. I was presenting to her my very own heart. Inside was the greatest gift I could give her as a mother-in-law.

Charele's small dainty fingers fumbled with the tiny ivory ribbon. The tedious purple wrapping finally fell to the tabletop. Hesitantly, she lifted the tiny box lid. She pulled out my familiar long blue apron strings and sweetly rolled her eyes at me.

The enclosed note let her know that I had cut off my apron strings and he was hers... no strings attached! That was three decades ago.

Montana mothers, I have kept my promise that I would never interfere in their marriage. My ties were severed.

Of course, my son will always be my son... my only child since our other son has passed away. So, for me to completely let go was especially important. (An only child has a big calling. He or she is left to care about both parents' needs.)

"A mother holds her childrens' hands for a while, but their hearts forever."

Conclusion

APPRECIATE YOUR CHILDREN'S ABILITIES

'FORMER LIBBY TENNIS PLAYER HONORED FOR ACCOMPLISHMENTS' was the heading in our local newspaper recently.

Two months later, a laminated magazine with a featured article was mailed to our home: 'TRAVIS JOHNSON, A HEART FOR TENNIS'.

> While visiting Travis' home in Arkansas this past year, a quality invitation from United States Tennis Association was mailed him: Congratulations! The Chenal Country Club has been selected by the USTA Arkansas Awards Committee to receive the Member Organization of the Year Award. This is a great honor, and your organization is very deserving.

> You will be presented this award at the Hall of Fame and Awards Banquet …and so on with the details.

Our son Travis has excelled in tennis and has been presented with other prestigious awards from Arkansas, like Tennis Pro of the Year in 2005.

His passion for tennis came when he received the opportunity to hold a tennis racquet and hit the ball in his small-town club in Montana. He says, "The first time I hit a tennis ball this feeling went through the racquet, up my arm, and into my heart. It never left. And from that point on, my life was changed." He loves tennis and will tell you, "It all comes down to fitness, strategy, and mental toughness" …and he is up to the challenge.

Travis never hesitates to give credit for his success by remembering his high school coach, the late Herb Neils. According to Travis, Herb was a man who had vision and the drive to bring that vision to life. He wanted to pass on his passion for tennis regardless of difficult

Travis tennis

circumstances. Herb knew some kids couldn't afford lessons due our small town's hurting economy. Therefore, Herb often provided them jobs from mowing grass to feeding horses.

Travis hopes someday that he can come back to Montana, his home, and continue Herb Neil's legacy and offer the same opportunities he was offered as a kid.

Readers, no matter if our children are grown or young they all have interest, talents or abilities that make them unique! As parents, help recognize your child's and encourage them in whatever that gift may be. And be proud, because when they succeed, we do as well! It shows in our swelled hearts.

In conclusion, even our young Kevin was successful in his short life. He had artistic abilities. Here is a story:

Walking into our seven-year-old son Kevin's Parent Teacher Conference, I noticed the bright multi-colored wall to my immediate right. His teacher, Mrs. Thoreson, displayed pictures of parrots that students had painted. One was obviously best. Immediately I wondered why his teacher would intimidate these little learners by placing her painting smack-dab in the middle. Her artistic ability compared to theirs had to be discouraging.

The conference started out as usual. Graciously, Mrs. Thoreson assured me Kevin was very polite and not a behavioral problem, but his energy level created problems. He loved to talk and had difficulty listening and keeping focused. "His attention span is small." Confirming, "He's continually out of his seat wanting to do things other than his assignment, things like digging in the wastebasket for scraps of construction paper because he loves art. In fact, (pointing over on the wall) you can see his parrot stands out."

"Whoa! Swinging my head to take another look at the wall, I asked, "Kevin did that?" I knew he drew incredible snowmobiles and motorcycles while sitting in church.

"You should get him into a special art class. That is something he enjoys … and sits for!" Mrs. Thoreson, suggested.

Young Kevin's art ability had my attention, but it took me nearly a year to act upon her advice.

The next time I was nudged to notice his talent was during our community's local spring art show. Artist Todd Hilelman painted small birds, displayed in two and three inch frames, each priced with tiny stickers neatly showing 25⁻ (no dollar signs). Kevin stopped at his table, lingering longer than usual. Then to my surprise, digging in the pocket of his size 8 slim jeans, he pulled out coins, pointing to a particular framed bird, asking, "Do you only want a quarter for that? "

"No. Sorry. That means twenty-five dollars," Todd informed him.

Kevin stepped back from Todd's display, exclaiming, "Mommy, I can make money painting!"

Because that situation tugged on my heartstrings, it prompted me. I felt for Kevin. Success was so close he could taste it. That is when I put Mrs. Thoreson's advice into action.

Phoning a local artist, Loretta Erickson, I inquired if she would be interested in my eight-year-old son attending class. Loretta, who taught teenagers and adults, hesitantly assured me he was probably too young, his little fingers were still being formed. I then explained his teacher suggested I put him in private art classes. Loretta relented and said, "Bring him to one class along with a sample of his work." Her other concern was Kevin might feel uncomfortable in a room of talented teenagers.

At age eight, I took Kevin to his first art class. Upon dropping him off, he was apprehensive, but energized. Grabbing his portfolio he jumped out of the car, slammed the door and quickly disappeared. I knew his eagerness outweighed his uncertainty.

Picking Kevin up 2 hours later, I experienced my first Parent Teacher dream conference. Loretta raved, "He is ready! He is going to do alright in my class and the teens think he is cute."

Driving home from class, Kevin encouraged, "Mommy I want to surprise you and daddy, so don't ask, but you are going to love hanging my painting!"

"Oh brother," being a home decorator, I felt badly thinking, "Where am I going to hang snowmobiles and motorcycles in our home?" But to my surprise, as seen in the photos, Mount Saint Helens with Spirit Lake and Glacier Park were his choices.

A few months laster, the late Jeff Swennes, (his Mother was a local artist) called, asking Kevin if he'd paint a picture for him to buy. When Jeff picked up his mountain scene, he handed nine-year-old Kevin a $50 bill. He felt like an esteemed artist who had already gained notoriety.

Kevin's dream was then to be in Libby's upcoming 1982 April Art Show.

The previous March, one evening after our routine bedtime Bible story, Kevin stretched out on the bed with hands clasped behind his head. Staring into the ceiling, thinking deeply, he asked, "Mommy, what do you think heaven will be like?"

Contemplating, without much time to think, I suggested, "You go first. What do you think?"

"I think heaven will be like when we go to the carnival and do all the fun rides and don't want to ever, ever leave!" Kevin quickly responded, "Now your turn."

Lame as my answer was, the best I could say was, "I know my heaven will be in all pinks and blues because I love those colors."

Removing his hand from underneath his blond hair, Kevin immediately poked me in the ribs, giggling and correcting me biblically. "Mommy, shame on you! Don't you know in Revelation, the Bible says there are all kinds of color? Walls of stones of emeralds, gold, rubies" …and on and on he went until I tickled him back so hard he squealed and fell off the bed.

Within a few weeks, life changed drastically for our family. Kevin needed a routine appendectomy. However, coming out of surgery, he suffered two cardiac arrests. Doctors revived him twice. They flew him to a bigger hospital. But later that week he died. Kevin's autopsy showed he had stomach cancer.

Libby's Art Show asked to display his paintings, recognizing his young talent. We felt honored. When picking up his last painting, I knew it was suppose to be my upcoming Mother's Day gift. His teacher Loretta explained through tears, his previous paintings had all been acrylic, but this was his first oil and he was not quite finished, but also it was his first real attempt to paint a sky.

When handed his last painting, a floodgate could not have held back my tears when I saw he'd painted the heavens in pink and blue! No one knew Kevin's and my previous conversation. Not even my husband, until later. In fact, I'd forgotten. But God reminded me in His perfect timing. Now I was holding the scene of where Kevin had gone.

My husband had Kevin's first painting etched on his headstone, along with Psalms 116:15, "Precious in the sight of the Lord is the death of his

Kevin's paintings when he was 8 and 9 years old

saints."

Looking back, encouraging Kevin's young artistic ability was meaningful and productive in his short life. His gifted talent became a part of our healing.

End

Made in the USA
Coppell, TX
28 February 2021